D0455008

Donated in Memory of
Mr. Richard A. Freedman

THE GRAD'S GUIDE TO

MONEY

Simple Tips to Saving, Giving, and Smart Spending

Matt Bell

TH1NK
TH1NK, an
Imprint of
NavPress

NAVPRESS

Discipleship Inside Out®

NavPress is the publishing ministry of The Navigators, an international Christian organization and leader in personal spiritual development. NavPress is committed to helping people grow spiritually and enjoy lives of meaning and hope through personal and group resources that are biblically rooted, culturally relevant, and highly practical.

**For a free catalog go to www.NavPress.com
or call 1.800.366.7788 in the United States or 1.800.839.4769 in Canada.**

ISBN-13: 978-1-61291-291-2
ISBN-13: 978-1-61291-456-5 (electronic)

Cover design by Arvid Wallen
Cover photo by Andrey Armyagov, Shutterstock

Some of the anecdotal illustrations in this book are true to life and are included with the permission of the persons involved. All other illustrations are composites of real situations, and any resemblance to people living or dead is coincidental.

Bell, Matt, 1960-
 The grad's guide to money : simple tips to saving, giving, and smart spending / Matt Bell.
  p. cm.
 ISBN 978-1-61291-291-2
 1. College graduates–Finance, Personal. 2. Finance, Personal–Religious aspects–Christianity. I. Title.
 HG179.B3724 2013
 332.024–dc23

                          2012036406

Printed in the United States of America

1 2 3 4 5 6 7 8 / 18 17 16 15 14 13

Other Books by Matt Bell

Money, Purpose, Joy

Money, Purpose, Joy Personal Workbook

Money, Purpose, Joy Discussion Guide

Matt Bell's Money Strategies for Tough Times

Money and Marriage

Freed-Up from Debt

Contents

CHAPTER 1: Your Future Is Amazingly Bright   7

CHAPTER 2: The Habits of Financial Wisdom   13

CHAPTER 3: Habit One: Remembering Who You Are   27

CHAPTER 4: Habit Two: Planning to Succeed   43

CHAPTER 5: Habit Three: Learning to Earn   59

CHAPTER 6: Habit Four: Giving Some Away   73

CHAPTER 7: Habit Five: Putting Some Away   87

CHAPTER 8: Habit Six: Avoiding the Big D   97

CHAPTER 9: Habit Seven: Managing Your Number   113

CHAPTER 10: Habit Eight: Playing Great Offense   125

CHAPTER 11: Habit Nine: Playing Great Defense   141

CHAPTER 12: Habit Ten: Spending Smart   149

CHAPTER 13: Living a Nonconforming Life   163

Appendix   175

Notes   179

About the Author   183

1

Your Future Is Amazingly Bright

"I know the plans I have for you," declares the LORD, "plans to prosper you and not to harm you, plans to give you hope and a future."

JEREMIAH 29:11

I'm doing all right, getting good grades. The future's so bright, I gotta wear shades.

TIMBUK3

You are very unusual. Did you know that?

It's highly unusual — some might even say *odd* — for a person your age to pick up a book about money. Even odder to actually *read* one.

But here's the really cool thing about your strange behavior. If you continue reading this book and actually put its ideas into practice, you are very likely to become oddly successful.

I make that claim with complete confidence because the principles in this book are not principles I made up. They are all drawn from the timeless truths of God's Word.

He cares so much about how you and I use money that he filled his Word with more counsel on money than on any other topic other than the kingdom of heaven.

You Have Huge Financial Potential

Over the course of your lifetime, you will likely handle several million dollars. That might seem impossible to believe since you probably don't have much money right now, but it's true that you have every possibility of earning and accumulating several million dollars.

Just flash-forward a few years. Imagine that you've graduated from college and have started working at a job for a very realistic $30,000 per year. Of course, you'll work hard, so now imagine that your hard work is rewarded with at least a 3 percent raise each year. By the time you're sixty-five years old, you will have earned almost $2.7 million!

Of course you're going to need to *spend* a lot of that money. You'll need a place to live, a car, food, clothing, the occasional vacation, and all the rest.

But let's say you make the really smart decision to live within your means—to spend less than you make. And now let's say you're super smart and choose to invest 10 percent of all the money you earn. By the time you're sixty-five, assuming you earn an average of 7 percent interest each year on the money you invest, you would have an investment account worth over $1.8 million.

Wow. You're a millionaire in the making!

Accumulating that much money in your lifetime won't even be all that difficult. You won't need a degree in finance, you won't need to work on Wall Street, and you won't need to win the lottery. You'll just need to do a lot of little things right for a long period of time.

Yet very few people come anywhere close to accumulating that much money.

Missed Opportunities

Consider this:

- Instead of the million dollars or more they realistically could have accumulated, half of all of today's workers age fifty-five or older have less than $50,000 saved for their retirement.[1] When they were your age, they had all the time and opportunity that you have, but they made very little of either one. After working for more than thirty years, they have left themselves in a very vulnerable position. Many will have to keep working long after they would have wanted to slow down. Others will be dependent on their adult children to help them out.
- Instead of adding happiness to people's lives, money often gets in the way, adding stress and messing with many people's most important relationships. Divorce attorneys say that financial issues are among the most common reasons couples split apart.
- Unfortunately, many people don't have to wait very long before they start feeling some financial pain. Many recent

college grads say money problems (usually the high monthly cost of paying back student loans) have led them to follow a career path other than the one they studied for. Their debts forced them to choose a job that paid the most instead of pursuing what they were passionate about. Many other recent college grads say they've had to put off grad school, delay when they'd like to get married, and wait longer than they'd prefer to buy a house, all because of financial problems.[2]

Why is that? With so much financial potential, why do so few people barely even scratch the surface of their potential? And what can *you* do to fulfill *yours*?

A Different Path

To a great degree, the answer is that most people follow our culture's teaching on money. They see what most people do with money, assume that's the right approach, and blindly march along.

Achieving true financial success will require that you take a different approach. It'll require that you live as you were intended to live, making decisions based on God's wisdom.

God's teaching on money can help everyone, but you are in an especially good stage of life to get more than most people from such teaching. That's because you have something going for you that older people don't have: time. God willing, you have many years ahead of you.

As will become clearer in chapter 10, when we talk about

investing, time is one of the most important raw ingredients for financial success. If you do little things right over a long period of time—if you build the right habits—you will be unusually successful.

There are plenty of older people today who would give anything for the chance to reset the clock and make better use of their time and money. This book will teach you the practical daily money-related habits, along with the important habits of the heart, that will help you make the most of the time and money that have been entrusted to you.

More Than Money

Biblical teaching about money is certainly about using money effectively: building savings, avoiding what it describes as the bondage of debt, and such. But God is interested in much more than just your *financial* success.

In the world, success is its own destination. Not so in the Bible, which tells us that to whom much is given, much is expected.

Taking a biblical approach to money is about putting God's principles into practice so that his purposes for your life and for the money he entrusts to you are fulfilled.

It's about using money in a way that leaves you free to hear and respond to God's call on your life, strengthens your most valuable relationships, enhances your relationship with God, and glorifies him.

It's an unusual approach to money, both counterintuitive and countercultural. As you'll see in the next chapter, I discovered

God's approach to money only after many years of foolishly following the world's financial plan.

At the end of each chapter, you'll find a verse of Scripture that I encourage you to memorize, a question or two for reflection or perhaps discussion with a friend, and a suggested action step. Throughout the book, you'll also find several forms or suggested websites to help you act on what you're learning. Combined, these features will help you establish the financial and spiritual habits that will last for years to come.

Memory Verse

"I know the plans I have for you," declares the LORD, "plans to prosper you and not to harm you, plans to give you hope and a future." (Jeremiah 29:11)

Reflection Questions

1. What's your reaction to the idea that you could very well end up earning and accumulating several million dollars in your lifetime? Is that exciting? Intimidating? Why?
2. What are some ways you could use that money to glorify God?

Action Step

Ask two people at least twenty years older than you what they wish they had done differently financially when they were your age.

2

The Habits of Financial Wisdom

If anyone loves me, he will obey my teaching.

JOHN 14:23

We are what we repeatedly do. Excellence, then, is not an act but a habit.

ARISTOTLE

The media is filled with stories of "overnight successes," but overnight success is a myth. In fact, writer Malcolm Gladwell has even quantified exactly what it takes to succeed in any field. In his book *Outliers,* he says that success—whether becoming a great grade-school teacher or an accomplished pianist—takes about ten thousand hours of practice.[1]

When it comes to successful money management, something very similar is true. I don't know that after ten thousand hours we'll all have the money thing completely figured out, but it is absolutely true that financial success comes through the cultivation and daily, ongoing practice of certain habits—practical habits and habits of the heart.

Habits Beat Circumstances

What you do with money on a regular basis—how well you do your job, how much you save or invest, how well you research various purchases, and how you think about money—will either lead you to a successful experience with money or not.

The day-to-day money-management habits you're building right now, at a time of life when you probably don't have much money, are hugely important. That's because once you *do* have some money, those habits will be magnified. And your circumstances matter a lot less than you may think.

No matter whether you scored high or low on your SAT or ACT, whether you major in education or nuclear physics, whether you become self-employed or work for someone else, whether your parents are rich or poor, whether you end up working outside or in an office, whether you live in a big city or a small town, whether you come from a white family, a black family, or a family of some other race, no matter what your circumstances, you have the potential to do extremely well financially.

I'm not saying your circumstances don't matter at all. Sure, if your parents pay for all of your schooling, you *may* have an easier time getting ahead financially than someone who graduates with $100,000 of student loan debt. *Maybe*, but not always.

There are plenty of people who had what looked like great circumstantial advantages over others and ended up far worse off.

By the same token, there are plenty of people who seemed to have all the cards stacked against them but went on to achieve remarkable success.

Habits are the great equalizer. A kid from a wealthy family who gets an MBA from a prestigious private school, spends a semester studying in France, and lands a high-paying job right out of school can easily fall into the habit of spending more than she makes.

A kid from a poor family who gets a degree in social work from a state school, never travels more than fifty miles from home on vacation, and starts out earning what most would agree is a meager salary can just as easily get in the habit of saving and investing a portion of all he makes.

Who will be more financially successful? I'm betting on the kid from the poor family.

In the chapters that follow, I'm going to introduce you to ten financial habits that will help you achieve financial success. Along the way, I'm going to challenge you regarding what you believe about money, because your belief system—habits of your heart and mind—will make all the difference in whether you actually put the more tangible financial habits into practice. And they hold the key to achieving not only financial success but *meaningful* financial success.

As I said earlier, the financial habits you start cultivating and practicing right now at your young age are hugely important because they will be magnified later in life. That's a lesson I learned the hard way.

Stumbling Toward Financial Success

I've been interested in money, especially *making* money, ever since I was old enough for my first paper route. I didn't get interested in learning how to *manage* money, though, until I had *mismanaged* a lot of money.

For as long as I can remember, I've been an extremely hard worker. I didn't just have a paper route, I had a *huge* paper route, and it enabled me to make some really good money for a twelve-year-old kid.

At other times when I was growing up, I mowed lawns, worked in cornfields (I grew up in a small town about an hour west of Chicago), cooked in restaurants, and shoveled snow. If there was an opportunity to earn some money, I was all over it.

A story my dad liked to tell was about a time when I was shoveling our long driveway on one brutally snowy day. Barely halfway into the job, a neighbor across the street got my attention and offered to pay me twenty dollars to shovel his driveway. Apparently, I immediately stopped working on our driveway and headed across the street.

Not exactly a great lesson in honoring my parents or following through on my commitments, but it spoke volumes about how hungry I was to earn money.

While I was really intent on *making* as much money as I could, I was also a superstar at *spending* money. I bought a small motorcycle when I was fourteen, got my first car right after I got my driver's license, bought a great car stereo, and found countless other ways to spend whatever I earned.

I never showed any interest in saving money. None. And the idea of investing? Not on my radar screen at all. I was all about making money and spending money.

Paper or Plastic?

When I got out of college, I discovered credit cards and thought they were amazing. The idea of buying things I wanted and then paying for only a small fraction of what I had bought each month seemed like a great deal.

I don't remember paying any attention to the amount of interest I was shelling out. All that mattered was that small monthly payment. Buy a lot, pay a little. Sounded good to me.

Credit cards helped me step up from merely spending *everything* I made each month to now being able to spend *more* than I made. And I did, quickly building balances on several credit cards.

A few years later, when I was twenty-five, I got a life-changing phone call. An uncle of mine had passed away and left me some money in his will. Sixty grand! I couldn't believe it. I had no idea he intended to leave me any money.

At the time, I was making about $25,000 a year working as a radio reporter in New Orleans, so to get a check for more than two years' worth of wages seemed like all the money in the world. I felt like I had won the lottery and I hadn't even bought a ticket.

Living My Dream

I had about three months between the time when I found out about the inheritance and when I actually received the money, so I had some time to think about what I would do with that money. And believe me, I spent *a lot* of time thinking about what I would do with that money.

Did I use it to pay off my credit card debts? Are you kidding?

While I was waiting for the check to show up, I read an article about a guy who loved France and so he created a newsletter about France. Once a month, he went there, traveled around, saw the sights, stayed at different hotels, ate at new restaurants, wrote some reviews, took some pictures, and published his newsletter.

Thousands of people subscribed to his newsletter. The article included a picture of him smiling happily in front of his nice house. It looked like he was living the life.

I decided that's what I would do: take my journalism skills and create a newsletter about something I loved. I was really into golf at the time and loved to travel, so I came up with a newsletter for people who take golf vacations. And while it lasted, it was a blast.

I would travel for seven to ten days every month, writing about, photographing, and, of course, playing some of the world's best golf courses. I played Pebble Beach on California's Monterey Peninsula, just about every golf course on the island of Puerto Rico, the amazing courses along Spain's Costa del Sol, and many others.

When I wasn't traveling, I used my newfound wealth to sample some of Chicago's better restaurants and clothing stores. I was in my midtwenties and I was living the life.

Never mind the fact that I wasn't attracting many paid subscribers to my newsletter. That seemed like a minor detail. I had what felt like an endless supply of money in the bank, so I just kept going. I kept traveling, playing all those amazing golf courses, staying at incredible resorts, and enjoying all that Chicago had to offer when I was home.

Money School Is Now in Session

I soon discovered in very painful fashion one of the most important lessons about money: When you spend more than you make every month—in my case, a lot more—eventually that doesn't work out so well. In fact, it leads to financial jail.

About two years after inheriting the money, I literally woke up one day to the fact that I was in financial trouble. Big trouble. I spent not only every last bit of the $60,000 inheritance but also much more money—another $20,000 on my credit cards, to be precise—and was having a tough time paying for food and rent while also keeping up with the minimum-required payments on my credit cards.

I had become so accustomed to the life I was living and so blind to what was happening with my money that when the inheritance ran out, I kept funding my lifestyle on those credit cards I had gotten so comfortable using before getting the inheritance.

The financial habits I developed early in life—first spending all that I made, and then spending more than I made—became more and more magnified as I got my hands on more and more money.

A Change of Venues

At about the same time that I woke up to my financial reality, my parents started sensing that something wasn't quite right and invited me home for a little chat. They soon invited me to *move home* with them, which is what I did for six months.

I will always be thankful to my parents. They caught me as I steered my financial life off a cliff. Getting some relief from bills such as rent and food gave me the margin I needed to start turning things around.

However, to go from living the life to living in my parents' basement was brutal. For the first two months, I found out what it means to be depressed. I remember just looking forward to the nighttime, when I could close my eyes and sleep. I wanted to forget about what a mess I had made of things.

And I dreaded it when the sun would come up in the morning and I had to spend another long day facing up to what I had done — the way I had mismanaged my uncle's money and squandered my once-in-a-lifetime opportunity.

But one day I found the motivation to start turning things around. It was an innocent request from my dad that did it. He simply asked me to start helping out around the house a little more. He had every right to expect me to do my part, but there was something about that request that shook me out of my depression. I thought, *What in the world am I doing living at my parents' house? I shouldn't be setting their table and taking out their trash at my age.*

I went back to journalism, picking up any freelance assignment I could get. I worked nights, weekends, anytime, anywhere to get some money rolling in again.

I also decided that I was still young enough to learn how to manage money successfully, and I got busy figuring it out.

I checked out money-management books from the library, listened to financial radio programs, and watched personal-finance videos. I became a sponge for all things financial.

I discovered two really important things about money in that journey. First, learning *what to do* to be successful with money isn't really all that difficult. There are certain basic habits that anyone with income can put into practice and be successful.

The second lesson took me longer to learn. In fact, it's a lesson that no one ever fully learns. That second lesson started with the realization that successful money management takes more than knowledge. It takes certain habits of the heart and mind. It takes the cultivation of the right worldview.

You see, if information was all that was required to get the money thing right, we'd all be millionaires. Just about everything you need to know about what to do with money is readily available. Search on any financial topic, and within a matter of seconds, you can find fairly credible answers on the Internet.

Yet tons of people still struggle with money.

The first time I thought about that was a huge aha moment. Information about wise money management is in plentiful supply, yet people who struggle with money are in plentiful supply as well. Why is that? Why isn't information enough?

The Missing Piece

My time at my parents' house got me thinking about the big questions of life: What's my purpose? Where do I go from here?

Right about then, I received a phone call from a friend I knew in college that marked the beginning of a life-changing spiritual journey.

Wayne and I had been in the same broadcast journalism program and had worked together at a public radio station while we were students. I graduated a year ahead of him and moved out of state for a job, and we fell out of touch. When Wayne heard that financial problems had led me to move back home with my parents, which wasn't far from where he lived, he gave me a call. It turns out that during his last year in college, Wayne's faith had become the central part of his life.

I grew up in a family who rarely went to church. My father was a nonpracticing Jew, my mother a nonpracticing Catholic. They sort of canceled each other out spiritually.

Even though my dad had told my mom he would not marry her if she insisted on raising kids as Catholics, she somehow passed down to me her basic beliefs. I grew up believing that Jesus is the Son of God and in heaven, but that's about as far as it went; those beliefs had little influence over how I lived my life.

When Wayne and I got together to talk, he said some pretty bold things about the mess I had made of my finances: "The more you've leaned on your own understanding, Matt, the more things haven't worked out so well."[2] He also offered a few hopeful comments, such as, "God has a plan for your life."[3]

As I thought about it, I had to agree with his first statement, and his second one intrigued me. I had no idea what might be next, so the suggestion that someone *did* know got my attention. The combination of my respect for Wayne, his passion for his convictions, my circumstances, and the notion that there may be some plan for my life that I didn't know about made me want to learn more about matters of faith. While maintaining the skepticism of a journalist, I began reading the Bible. I even started going to church.

Eventually, I moved back to Chicago, living in a tiny studio apartment. I also started dating someone I met at church.

One night, after an upsetting argument that put the future of the relationship in doubt, I found myself in the quiet of my tiny apartment, feeling very broken. It was all-too similar to the feeling I had when my golf newsletter was going under. Wayne's words echoed in my head: *The more you've leaned on your own understanding, Matt, the more things haven't worked out so well*, and, *God has a plan for your life.*

I realized that I was still working *my* plan and, once again, it wasn't working out. I bowed my head and prayed a simple prayer: *God, if you really do exist, I'd like to know you. If you really do have a plan for my life, I'd sure like to know what it is. I'm sorry for the many ways I must have disappointed you and for making myself the focus of my life. From this point forward, my life is in your hands. Do with it what you will. Amen.*

Two Journeys Become One

I didn't see any lightning bolts, the clouds didn't part, and no weeping angels appeared. But after committing my life to Christ, I began to study the Bible more closely. The more I read it, the more I realized that it has a lot to say about money. A lot!

I also started to see that much of what I was learning about a life of faith was directly relevant to how I managed my finances. What I'd thought were two separate journeys — my financial journey and my spiritual journey — were tightly bound together.

One of my biggest discoveries was when I realized that many of the cultural messages about managing money are completely wrong. Instead of moving us toward greater success and happiness, they push us in the opposite direction. As I began helping others with their finances, I started seeing that our acceptance of the common beliefs about money management has turned many of us into prodigal sons and daughters, leading us away from home — home being a metaphor for all that truly matters and makes life meaningful.

Many financial teachers who want to help people move in a better direction with their money share a common recommendation — namely, to stop stretching so far. It's a reasonable-sounding idea, logical even, what with the savings rate and debt levels where they are. But it, too, is wrong. The real solution is that we need to stop settling for so little.

Pursuing meaningful financial success requires that we set our sights higher, that we become clear about what truly matters and who we were made to be. It involves looking beyond the many cultural distractions that seem intent on pulling us off course. It means keeping our eyes fixed and our money focused on that which gives our lives meaning, purpose, and joy and refusing to settle for anything less. When we use God's Word as our guide, our use of money becomes a powerful expression of who we are and what we're about.

Lasting behavioral changes require internal changes—changes in how we think and in what we believe. So that's the focus of the first habit, which we'll discuss in the next chapter. For a financial book, this is an uncommon approach. But I assume you're interested in uncommon results—not just the appearance of success but true and meaningful success.

Memory Verse

If anyone loves me, he will obey my teaching. (John 14:23)

Reflection Questions

1. What are some of your current financial habits? Try to identify at least two good financial habits and two that are not so good.
2. Where did you learn your current financial habits? Your parents? Your friends? The media?

Action Step

Start getting in the habit of keeping your receipts every time you spend money. I'll tell you what to do with them in chapter 4.

Habit One:
Remembering Who You Are

If anyone is in Christ, he is a new creation; the old has gone, the new has come!
2 CORINTHIANS 5:17

People need to be reminded more often than they need to be instructed.
SAMUEL JOHNSON

In the chapters ahead, I'm going to take you through several objective, knowledge-based steps toward wise money management. Start building these essential habits right now while you're in college and you'll be well on your way toward achieving remarkable financial success.

But knowing *what* to do isn't enough. We have to take action. Yet we're not robots that can be programmed to do the right thing every time.

We have feelings, emotions, and through our emotions, we can be all too easily manipulated, especially if we're not clear about the purpose of our lives. We can be persuaded to do things with money that are not in our best interests and, more important, not glorifying to God.

It Takes More Than How-To Information

When I first got interested in learning how to manage money well, I spent a lot of time gathering information. What's the best way to get out of debt? Buy a car? Invest? However, as I mentioned in the previous chapter, things didn't really begin to change for me until I noticed how strange it seemed that despite easy access to information about how to make all kinds of financial decisions well, money continues to be a challenge for a lot of people.

What's missing for many of us, I realized, is an understanding of the purpose of our lives. If we can dial down the noise of our culture long enough to figure out what really matters, that can guide us to the best use of money. In fact, it's our only hope.

It is only by understanding the purpose of our lives that we can understand the purpose of money. Only by orienting our financial priorities and daily financial decisions around a commitment to live the lives we were designed to live can we possibly fulfill our financial potential. It's the only path that leads to not only financial success but to *meaningful* financial success.

The thing is, a lot of us have forgotten who we were made to be.

The Greatest Identity Theft Ever

Identity theft, where someone steals your Social Security number or credit card information, has become a common crime, impacting an estimated fifteen million people each year. As bad as the problem is, about a hundred years ago, an identity theft took place on a far grander scale.

Everyone's identity was stolen.

Amazingly, this huge heist didn't make headlines, and it didn't prompt any calls for new legislation. In fact, no one even seemed to notice. And although every generation since has continued to be impacted by the Great Identity Robbery, very few people today are even aware of the problem.

What in the world am I talking about? I'm talking about the change in personal identity that happened during the Industrial Revolution. That's when we became *consumers.*

The consumer identity has been messing with our finances and our sense of self-worth ever since. Here's a brief look at how the deal came down.

A Short History of Our Consumer Culture

According to historian William Leach, author of *Land of Desire*, the foundation of our consumer culture was established roughly between the 1880s and 1920s.[1] That's when people moved en masse from the country to the city and took up positions along assembly lines that mass-produced branded versions of everything from cars to clothing.

The move from country to city marked far more than a change of address; it marked a change in people's way of life. They went from farm work to factory work, from making things to buying things.

And it marked a change in identity. As historian Susan Strasser wrote in *Satisfaction Guaranteed*, "Formerly *customers*, purchasing the objects of daily life from familiar craftspeople and storekeepers, Americans became *consumers*."[2]

Before that time, people usually bought raw materials in bulk; there were no branded packages of ready-to-eat cereal and not much in the way of ready-to-wear clothing. "People who had never bought corn flakes were taught to need them," Strasser explained. "Those formerly content to buy oats scooped from the grocer's bin were informed about why they should prefer Quaker Oats in a box."[3]

Manufacturing Desire

It was during the Industrial Revolution that department stores emerged, which, in turn, spawned the increasingly sophisticated science of merchandising. Store managers learned to display items with an eye toward enticement.

The expansion of railway lines helped create national markets. The spread of telegraph and telephone lines helped create national advertising. With more goods to sell and more markets to reach, more sophisticated techniques for driving desire were developed: psychological techniques.

Boston College sociology professor Juliet Schor, author of *The*

Overworked American, said the 1920s marked a clear turning point in the ad industry:

> Of course, ads had been around for a long time. But something new was afoot, in terms of both scale and strategy. . . . Ads developed an association between the product and one's very identity. Eventually they came to promise everything and anything — from self-esteem, to status, friendship, and love.[4]

Marketers began positioning the activities of consumption as being in the best interests of those doing the consuming. According to William Leach, "The cardinal features of this culture were acquisition and consumption as the means of achieving happiness"[5] and what religion historian Joseph Haroutunian called "'being' through 'having.'"

There's a scene in the movie *Confessions of a Shopaholic* that highlights this notion of "being through having." The lead character, Rebecca, walks into a high-end clothing boutique, lured in by a sign in the window indicating that a sale is taking place.

She admires a green scarf on a mannequin but walks away, telling herself, *Rebecca, you just got a credit card bill for $900. You do not need a new scarf.* As she turns away, the mannequin comes to life and says, "Then again, who *needs* a scarf? Wrap some old jeans around your neck. That'll keep you warm. That's what your mother would do."

Rebecca responds, "You're right. She would."

"The point about this scarf," the mannequin says, "is that *it would become part of the very definition of your psyche.*"

Now, of course, Rebecca *needs* that scarf. And in true

overspent, consumer fashion, when she goes to buy it, coming up with the money isn't so easy. She tries to cobble together enough by using a little cash, putting some on one nearly maxed-out credit card, some on another, and some on yet another. But the last card doesn't go through. With a smirk on her face, the salesclerk says, "Declined."[6]

What's in a Word?

Today, the use of the word *consumer* has become so common that most of us don't even notice. Every week, we hear about consumer spending, consumer sentiment, and consumer segments. We accept the label without question.

But consider this: To consume literally means to use up, squander, or spend wastefully. It's right there in the dictionary. How's that working out for us?

Consumer is more than a word; it's a worldview. I mean, think about it: If I'm a consumer, *who's* the most important person in the world? Me, right?

If I'm a consumer, *what's* most important to me? Money and things.

I would also argue that if I'm a consumer, I live with a competition mindset. I'm in competition with my neighbors and coworkers, my friends and relatives, to have more and better stuff than they have.

The acceptance of the consumer identity goes a long way toward explaining why so many people have too much debt, too little savings, too much financial stress, and too little contentment.

It helps explain why so many people live as if they're just one purchase away from happiness (*If only we could afford a better brand of clothing, a nicer car, a*—you fill in the blank).

It explains why people usually make spending their highest priority and then wonder why they never seem to have enough to save, invest, or give away.

Every day of your life, from the very beginning of your life, marketers have been busy doing their best to mold you into a consumer. And they're really good at it.

The Pull of the Culture

There's a cultural conversation about money that takes place every day. It's so prevalent, so woven into the fabric of our daily lives, that we hardly even notice anymore.

I don't believe that marketers or advertisers are bad people. But we need to know how marketing and advertising works.

Since the moment you entered the world, marketers have been trying to connect with you, make an impression on you, and mold how you think and how you spend. I don't mean to excuse any overspending people, but I do want to point out that there's a lot about our culture that encourages us to spend more than we have.

Chances are good that when you came home from the hospital, you were wearing a diaper with a cartoon character printed on it. It looks innocent enough, yet the company behind the cartoon character paid a lot of money to put that character on all those diapers, knowing its presence would help generate added sales. They knew you'd soon recognize that character, love that character, and want to own lots of other stuff plastered with that character's picture.

By eighteen months of age, the average child can identify logos. By the time that child hits first grade, she can identify more than two hundred brands.

And what's the message that's being communicated? What impact is all of that kid-targeted marketing having?

Let's check in with today's nine- to fourteen-year-olds. About one-third would rather spend time shopping than almost any other activity. Over half say that when you grow up, the more money you have, the happier you will be. And almost two-thirds agree that "the only kind of job I want when I grow up is one that will get me a lot of money."

The consumerist message tells us that things bring happiness and not to worry if you can't afford it: Just charge it.

Marketing Subtlety

It used to be that we noticed whenever a marketing message was communicated to us. There was a clear distinction between the TV program we were watching and the commercials. But now, with product placements a prominent part of many programs, the marketing is much more constant, much more subtle.

It used to be that advertising was something we could clearly see or hear: billboards, radio commercials, and such. But now, with word-of-mouth advertising and affiliate marketing, you never know whether the recommendation from a friend or favorite blogger is a paid pitch.

Stores are set up based on scientific studies of how people tend to navigate the space. The milk is put in the back of the store intentionally. It's a frequently purchased item. Making people go to the back of the store to get their gallon of milk increases the chances that they'll walk out with other stuff they had no intention of buying.

Products are arranged based on a scientific study of shoppers' eye movements. The more expensive items are typically at eye level. Apparently, we're less likely to buy the less-expensive stuff if we have to go through all the effort of looking up or down.

Marketers have learned that if you put the soup in alphabetical order, it makes people find what they're looking for more easily, and that's bad for sales. If people have to hunt around, chances are good they'll find something else that looks appealing and buy more.

It's the same thing with mail-order catalogs. Have you ever noticed that very few have a table of contents? You have to flip through them to find what you want. You buy more that way.

And don't worry if you can't afford it. More credit is always available.

The Consumer Treadmill

It's easy to become wrapped up in the cycle of consumerism. We work hard to earn money. Then we go home to watch TV and relax, and as we watch our shows and the commercials that come on, we're told we need certain products in order for us to truly be valuable. So we go to the store, buy the product, feel better for a little while, and the next day go back to work to pay for the thing we just bought. When we get home and are ready to relax, we turn on the TV or flip through a magazine and are told we're still not good enough, smart enough, or cool enough if we don't possess some other product. We just keep working and watching and buying . . . and working and reading and buying.

We're running on the consumer treadmill. And the thing about treadmills is that we can work up a huge sweat and wear ourselves out but never actually go anywhere. We end in the exact same place we began.

Chasing an Elusive Form of Happiness

There's been an interesting shift in the field of psychology in recent years. For a long time, psychologists were primarily interested in the causes of mental illness. But more recently, some have become very interested in the causes of mental wellness. It's a branch of psychology known as positive psychology: the scientific study of what leads to human happiness.

Positive psychologists say one of the biggest mistakes we make in our pursuit of happiness is to base our happiness on a relative scale. We gauge our happiness on a comparison with our neighbors, friends, coworkers, and relatives. What are they driving and where are they going on vacation? How do we stack up?

And we base our happiness on how we're doing today compared with how we were doing last month and last year, so we're constantly reaching for something that's a little bit beyond our grasp. We always seem to need a little more.

The psychologists call this the hedonic treadmill. We're running hard, we're pursuing something, but it's never enough. As Bono sings, we still haven't found what we're looking for.

A Better Track to Run On

Do you remember the three beliefs of a consumer? First is that you're the most important person in the world. Second is that money and things lead to happiness. And third is that life is a competition to have more and better stuff than other people, and more and better stuff than you used to have.

But positive psychologists say that's the exact wrong approach if it's a life of meaning and purpose we're after. They say that instead of living lives of competition, we should strive to live lives of contribution. We all have certain gifts, talents, and passions, and when we find a way to put them to use making a difference in the world, that contributes greatly to our sense of meaning.

Positive psychologists also say that if it's a life of meaning, purpose, and joy we're after, instead of loving money and material things, it's far better to love people. This may be intuitive, but there's also a lot of research showing that people who are in close, supportive, loving relationships are happier than those who aren't.

And perhaps the most important finding of positive psychologists is that if it's a life of meaning, purpose, and joy we're after, we shouldn't put ourselves at the center of our world. Arranging our use of money around those priorities—making a difference with our lives, building into our key relationships, and living for something bigger than us — is the key to achieving financial success that truly satisfies.

Surprise, Surprise

It's interesting but not surprising how well the findings of secular social scientists line up with what the Bible teaches.

Make a difference with your life? Absolutely. The Bible says each of us has been given "something to do that shows who God is" (1 Corinthians 12:6, MSG).

Love people? Jesus said that's the second greatest commandment (see Matthew 22:39).

But here's where the Bible differs from today's social scientists. Our lives are not just about living for some*thing* bigger than we are. The Bible says our lives are about living for some*one* bigger: God. The first and greatest commandment is to love God (see verses 34-38).

These are the three purposes of our lives: love God, love people, and make a difference. Therefore, they are the three purposes of money. When we use money to pursue these purposes, we discover that the whole money thing works best.

Made for So Much More

Clearly, living according to our culture is akin to settling for far too little. I don't know about the Bible you read, but the one I read does not say that on the sixth day, God made consumers who would use up, waste, and squander all that he made on the first five days. It says he made man and woman in his image.

Financially, our identity is that of a steward, but I think a lot of people misunderstand that. The word seems heavy, like a burden. It's as if they've been given managerial responsibility over some stuff and misheard the instructions as "Whatever you do, don't break or lose any of this stuff."

Those aren't the instructions we've been given at all.

In the parable of the talents (see Matthew 25:14-30), a wealthy man entrusts three servants with his stuff, goes on a long journey, and then returns to see how they did. One servant got the instructions wrong. He hid what was entrusted to him and then returned it to his master. He hadn't lost or broken any of it, but for his efforts, or lack thereof, he received a harsh rebuke.

The other two servants were different. They turned what had been entrusted to them into something more. For their efforts, they received strong words of affirmation. Oh, and on top of that, the master then entrusted them with more.

Of course, the master represents God; the servants represent us.

Embracing our identity and pursuing our purposes aren't things we can easily check off our to-do lists. It's not as simple as opening a savings account. It's about opening our heart every day to God.

It takes daily time in the Word. It takes being part of a community of believers. It takes being in prayerful conversation with God throughout each day.

You can learn all the techniques in the world about successful money management. You may be seen as smart and effective.

But in order to be wise, you must always remember who you are.

You're a child of God and a steward of all he has generously entrusted to your care. You have been given the responsibility — the opportunity, really — to use God's resources in ways that glorify him, strengthen your most valuable relationships, and enable you to make a difference with your life.

Remembering your identity and the purposes of your life is the first habit to develop if you want to achieve meaningful success.

Memory Verse

If anyone is in Christ, he is a new creation; the old has gone, the new has come! (2 Corinthians 5:17)

Reflection Questions

1. What are some of the core marketing messages you hear on a regular basis, and how have those messages influenced some of your financial decisions?
2. How are the messages and your decisions either in synch with or at odds with your biblical identity and the three key purposes of your life?

Action Step

Start to notice every time you hear or read the word *consumer*. Each time you do, consciously reject that label and remind yourself that you are more than that. If you've placed your faith in

Christ, the Bible says you are "a child of God" (see John 1:12). Financially, you are a steward—one who has been placed in a position of responsibility over the management of the resources God has generously entrusted to your care (see Genesis 2:15,19-20).

4

Habit Two:
Planning to Succeed

The plans of the diligent lead to profit as surely as haste leads to poverty.

PROVERBS 21:5

It's easy to meet expenses — everywhere we go, there they are.

ANONYMOUS

I f you were going to build a house, you wouldn't just show up at the job site with a hammer, some nails, and some two-by-fours and start pounding boards together, would you? No. You'd have a plan, a blueprint. There's no way you'd be able to build a decent house without one.

The same is true of your financial life. You need a plan. Of course, I'm talking about a tool that makes people yawn, roll their eyes, cringe, or worse. I'm talking about a budget.

An Image Problem

Be honest. What went through your mind when you read the word *budget*? Probably not joyful thoughts.

I know that using a budget is one of the most boring-sounding, unpleasant financial ideas in the world. People think of a budget as a financial killjoy, something that will take all the fun out of life.

When I teach workshops, I like to ask people, "If a budget were a person, who would it be?" Answers usually include Scrooge and the Grinch. One person said Darth Vader; another even associated a budget with the Devil.

One married guy said his mother-in-law came to mind. I don't know what happened in that relationship, but I don't think it was good.

Clearly, budgets have an image problem.

A lot of people seem to think of a budget as something you *go on*, like a diet. "Poor Bob," they say. "He's on a budget." Or they think a budget is only for people who need one, like people trying to dig out from under a mountain of debt.

But a budget isn't something you *go on*; it's a tool you use in order to get the most from your money. You may have to take this on faith, but a budget is the single-most-powerful tool any of us can use for wise, effective, even joyful money management.

Budgets are for everyone—that is, everyone who wants to achieve uncommon financial success. In one of my favorite secular personal-finance books, *The Millionaire Next Door*, authors Thomas Stanley and William Danko point out that more than half of all millionaires use a budget to plan their spending.[1] If ever there were someone who didn't need a budget, it would be a millionaire, right? Wrong. They call it one of the essential keys to financial success.

If you have any money coming in each month, use a plan to decide ahead of time what to do with that money.

Setting Fences

Let me tell you a short story that should help you see budgets in a more positive light. It's the story of a grade school that was built close to a busy road. The kids at this school were kind of unusual because when the recess bell rang, they weren't too eager to go out and play. They'd been warned time and time again by their teachers and parents to stay away from the busy road.

Many of those kids just stayed close to the school building during recess out of fear. They missed out on all the fun. Of the kids who ventured out onto that scary playground, every now and then there would be a close call, as a kid would lose sight of the boundaries of the playground while chasing a ball.

Finally someone had the bright idea to put up a fence, and suddenly the kids were free to run throughout the full expanse of that playground to their hearts' delight. The clearly marked boundary freed them up to play without worry.

That's how a budget, or, as I prefer, a *Cash Flow Plan*, works. You set the fences in your various spending categories so you know where it's safe to spend.

While a lot of people who don't use a *Cash Flow Plan* think it would be like strapping a ball and chain to their leg, the reality is that using one isn't restrictive; it's freeing.

When you want to buy some clothes, you look to see how much money you have left in your clothing budget this month and you're free to spend that full amount. As you spend the money, you have peace of mind. You know that the amount you're spending is part of a plan that also enables you to buy other things, be generous, save, and live with financial margin.

The Good That Budgets Can Do

When you know how much you have left to spend on entertainment before you go out on a Friday night, you are free to spend that money. You won't drag any nagging questions into the movie theater about how splurging on a crate-sized container of popcorn may impact your ability to buy some new clothes the next day.

A *Cash Flow Plan* works especially well when you link it to specific financial goals you're trying to achieve.

Look at the four quadrants in the chart on page 47. If you don't have goals and don't have a plan (the lower-right quadrant), you are wandering. You don't know where you want to go and you've got no plan for getting there. Good luck with that!

If you don't have goals, but you do have a plan (lower-left quadrant), you may be obsessing over your finances. You're keeping tabs over the details of your finances but with no real purpose or destination in mind. People who are fanatically frugal tend to fall into this camp, often thinking they can't afford this or that when maybe they can.

If you have goals but no plan (upper-right quadrant), you may be dreaming. You have a vision for where you'd like to go but no plan for getting there. This comes with regular disappointments and frustrations. You have high hopes but never seem to achieve the goals you have in mind.

Lastly, if you have goals and a plan (upper-left quadrant), you are truly *managing* money. This is the steward's quadrant.

Goal Quadrant

	Cash Flow Plan	**No Cash Flow Plan**
Goals	Managing	Dreaming
No Goals	Obsessing	Wandering

Take a minute to mark the quadrant you think fits your current habits. You might even list a few reasons you chose the quadrant you did. Honestly assessing where you are now will help you prepare a successful plan later.

Flexibility Built In

A *Cash Flow Plan* is just what it sounds like: a *plan* you develop that predetermines what you will do with any money that comes your way. When you decide ahead of time how much you will give and save and how much you can afford to spend on clothing, entertainment, and everything else, there's no reason to worry.

This chapter will teach you how to set up and use a *Cash Flow Plan* and then walk you through three options for putting your plan into action.

My goal is to help you see that a budget is not about *less*, as in spending less in every category; it's about *more*, as in having more knowledge about where your money is going. Once you know exactly how you're using your money now, you can be more effective in choosing where it should go later so you have more for what matters most.

A Cash Flow Plan How-To Guide

Here are the four steps for successfully setting up and using a *Cash Flow Plan*.

1. Estimate current income and expenses.
2. Plan future income and expenses.
3. Monitor actual income and expenses.
4. Review and revise.

1. Estimate current income and expenses.
The first step in developing a *Cash Flow Plan* is to estimate your current income and expenses. Go ahead and fill in the "Now" columns on the *Cash Flow Plan*. An example of the form is on page 176. You can also download full-sized forms for free from SoundMindInvesting.com in the resources section.

Some of the categories will be easy to complete. You know your fixed expenses, such as your cell phone bill (assuming you stick to your allotted minutes). However, you might not know how much you spend each month on entertainment or clothing. That's okay. For now, just take an educated guess.

For expenses or bills that occur less often than monthly, such as a semiannual vehicle-insurance premium, take the annual amount you spend, divide by twelve, and enter that amount. Be sure to include at least $25 per month for "Miscellaneous" since there are always expenses that don't fit neatly into one of the preplanned categories.

In the bottom-right corner of the form, subtract your total estimated monthly outgo from your total estimated monthly income (money earned at a part-time job, spending money your parents provide, and so on).

2. Plan future income and expenses.

Next, fill in the "Goal" columns for your monthly income and expenses. I'll give you some specific recommendations about how to allocate that money across the various *Cash Flow Plan* categories in just a minute.

3. Monitor actual income and expenses.

The third step is to track where your money *actually* goes. There are three main ways to do this: the envelope system, a paper-and-pencil system, or an electronic system. As you read the following descriptions, see which one best suits you.

The envelope system. (Best for people who prefer to use cash whenever possible. Also a really good hands-on system that gives you clear feedback on how well you're managing your plan.) Each time you receive money, fill envelopes with the amount of cash you have budgeted for specific spending categories until the next time you are paid. For instance, if you have a part-time job that pays you once a month and have $50 budgeted for clothing, each time you get paid, put $50 in cash into an envelope labeled "clothing."

When you go shopping for clothes, take that envelope with you, pay for your clothing with the money in the envelope, and put the change back in the envelope. Write down on the outside of the envelope how much you spent, the date, where you spent it, and what it was for. This record will come in handy at the end of each month. You'll be able to analyze where you spent your money and see if you'd like to make any changes next month.

When you're out of money in a certain envelope, you're done spending in that category until your next payday.

Paper-and-pencil system. (Best for people who use a combination of cash, debit/credit cards, and online bill pay.) Track your spending by keeping receipts or by writing down how much you spend during the day, and then enter that information on the *Cash Flow Tracker* at the end of each day. There's an example of this form on page 177. (You can download full-sized copies from SoundMindInvesting.com.)

Across the top of the *Cash Flow Tracker*, enter your income and expense goals from the *Cash Flow Plan*. The reason there are not enough rows for every day of the month is because you aren't likely to spend money in every category every day, so the rows underneath "Goals" are not meant to represent each day of the month. The column underneath "Goals" is for whatever notes you may want to add. Perhaps you'd like a reminder that a gift expense was for Uncle Frank or that an entertainment expense was for a movie.

The numbers across the bottom of the form represent the days of the month. This can help you remember to write down your daily expenses. People new to the budgeting process sometimes forget to write down their spending for a day or two. As they lose track of their spending, they become frustrated and give up. Crossing off today's date at the bottom of the form after entering the day's spending lets you know you've recorded all of your expenses for the day.

At the end of the month, total up each category and then indicate how much over or under your actual spending was compared to the goal. Because you will use one form for each month, look at the previous month's *Cash Flow Tracker* to see how much over or under you were up to that point in the year, and enter that on this month's form. Then total up how much over or under you are for the year.

An electronic system. There are three main electronic systems:

- *Excel spreadsheet.* (Best for people who like the layout of the paper-and-pencil system but prefer to use an electronic tool.) On the Sound Mind Investing website, you'll find downloadable Excel spreadsheets formatted just like the paper-and-pencil *Cash Flow Plan* and *Cash Flow Tracker.* This can simplify some aspects of the paper-and-pencil system by totaling your columns automatically.
- *Budget software.* (Best for people who are computer savvy and like lots of detail in their budgets.) Quicken is the main game in town. After buying the software, load it onto a computer via a disc or download the program online. Quicken can download your checking, savings, and credit card transactions through an online connection with your bank or credit union and credit card companies.

    One downside to budget software is the cost. Another is that it tethers you to one computer. You can access your *Cash Flow Plan* information only on the computer where the software is installed. To overcome these issues, let's look at the third category of electronic tools.
- *Online tools.* (Best for people who are comfortable doing online banking, prefer to have their *Cash Flow Plan* available online, and don't need a ton of detail.) These are the newest players in the electronic budgeting space. The main provider is Mint (Mint.com).

The creation of free online budget tools, along with their smartphone apps, has helped give budgets something of a makeover. They've taken a lot of the pain out of the budgeting process and have even made it something close to fun to see where your money goes each month.

They automatically track most of your spending — your credit card and debit card purchases, the checks you write. The only thing you have to enter manually is your use of cash. You can indicate how much you intend to spend in various categories and then quickly see how much you've actually spent at any point in time.

The first step in using an online budget tool can be the most unnerving: You have to enter your bank and credit card passwords. The leading providers know that people's number one concern is security, so they go to the nth degree in making sure their systems are secure. Still, if you're not comfortable with this, use one of the other systems rather than an online one.

Once you are set up to allow the service to access your records, it will download your latest transactions automatically. It can also be set up to automatically categorize certain transactions for you. For example, if you go out to eat at a certain restaurant on a regular basis, you can tell the service to always categorize those transactions as entertainment.

Mint makes its money by recommending the services of paid clients. For example, in order to use the tool, you have to say where you have a checking or savings account and what types of credit cards you use. If one of Mint's sponsors has a better deal—maybe they pay more interest on checking—Mint might recommend that you check out that company. But the recommendations are not at all intrusive, and I think it's a small price to pay for a good service.

We use Mint in our household and trust that it's secure.

If you are new to budgeting, I recommend that you use a manual system, such as the envelope system or the paper-and-pencil system, for at least the first year. It will give you more of a hands-on feel for the budgeting process. Once you get comfortable with budgeting, then you could switch to an electronic system.

4. Review and revise.

Finally, look at your actual cash flow compared to your plan. Do this evaluation at the end of every month.

If you are way off in a certain category, one of two things is probably true. First, you weren't proactive enough in managing to stay within the number. Perhaps you knew the monthly target for a certain category but never checked to see how much of the budget was left until the end of the month, and by that time you had overspent the category. You'll need to spend less in the months ahead to catch up, and you'll need to get in the habit of checking to see how you're doing before spending more in a category.

Second, your budget target in one or more categories was unrealistic. Maybe you need to plan to spend more on clothing than you thought, which will mean you'll have to plan to spend less in a different category.

Setting Your Financial Priorities

Now let's get more specific in setting up your plan. There are only five things you can do with money once you have some. You can:

1. Spend it.
2. Use it for debt payments.
3. Save it.
4. Invest it.
5. Give it away.

And that's the typical order, the one most people follow. We start earning some money and our first thoughts are all about spending. What sort of clothing can we buy? What can we afford to do for fun this weekend? Where can we go for spring break?

What I've discovered is that when spending comes first, it usually comes with debt payments, such as credit card balances. A spend-first approach to money makes it practically impossible to live within our means, so that's why making debt payments is a high priority.

Next, if there's any money left over, some might be saved or invested, and maybe a little will even be given away. But there usually isn't much, if any, money left over.

Here's a much better way to prioritize your use of money. For every dollar you bring in — whether through a part-time job, a summer job, or money your parents give you — give some away, and then save or invest some right off the top. If you have debt, that will have to come next, but if you don't have debt, keep it that way.

Then—after you've given some away, saved or invested some, and made your debt payments—you can decide how much you can afford to spend on entertainment, clothing, vacations, and such.

This is a very simple but very powerful idea. Giving and then saving or investing portions of all that you receive before deciding how much to spend will be hugely helpful to you in achieving uncommon financial success.

In the chapters ahead, we'll take a look at each of these priorities in more detail.

Things to Keep in Mind

New habits take time to build. Realize you may take a couple of steps backward for every step forward. Give yourself some grace and stick with it. Eventually, you'll wonder how you ever did the money thing without a plan.

Don't make the use of a *Cash Flow Plan* your goal. No one is excited about that. Instead, determine to use money in a God-glorifying way and save enough to be able to start your post-college life really well. Then use a *Cash Flow Plan* as a key means to accomplish your goals. In the following chapters, you'll be setting specific goals for the various categories on the *Cash Flow Plan*.

Memory Verse

The plans of the diligent lead to profit as surely as haste leads to poverty. (Proverbs 21:5)

Reflection Questions

1. How do you feel about the idea of using a *Cash Flow Plan*? If you're not thrilled about the idea, what are some reasons why?
2. How does thinking about yourself as a steward, or manager, of God's resources impact the way you think about using a *Cash Flow Plan*?

Action Step

Decide which cash flow tracking system you will use: the envelope system, a paper-and-pencil system, or one of the electronic systems. No matter which system you choose, use the *Cash Flow Plan* worksheet to estimate your monthly income and expenses. Then start tracking your daily use of money.

Habit Three:
Learning to Earn

Whatever you do, work at it with all your heart, as working for the Lord, not for men.

COLOSSIANS 3:23

Work while you have the light. You are responsible for the talent that has been entrusted to you.

HENRI-FRÉDÉRIC AMIEL

Do you remember the fable "The Goose That Laid the Golden Egg"? A couple owned an amazing goose that produced a golden egg every day. But soon one golden egg a day wasn't enough; they wanted more. So, assuming that the inside of the bird must be made out of gold, they cut it open only to discover nothing but a bunch of goose guts. That, of course, marked the end of their daily dose of gold.

Your ability to generate income is like that goose. Take care of that ability, and it will take care of you.

And this isn't just about the work you'll do after graduating from college. It's also about your schoolwork, volunteer work, an internship, and any part-time paid work you do during college.

Working During School

About half of today's full-time college students also hold part-time jobs. That has a lot to do with the high cost of college. However, working while going to school can help you do more than pay the bills. It can help you test out jobs you may want to pursue after college and cultivate work habits that will serve you well in your future full-time job. If you choose a part-time job in the field you'd like to go into after graduation, the connections you make can also help you land a full-time job when you're ready.

You won't want to work so many hours that your job negatively impacts your grades. In part, that depends on how rigorous your coursework is, but it also depends on how many hours you work. Research shows that working more than twenty hours per week *does* typically have a negative impact on school performance. In part, it depends on whether the job is on or off campus. Students working on campus usually achieve better grades, whereas students working off campus typically end up with lower grades.[1]

Money-Making Opportunities While You're in School

One of the best jobs I had in school was working at a restaurant. It wasn't a career path I wanted to pursue after graduation, but I made lots of friends with coworkers, and as an often-hungry college student, the benefit of free meals was huge!

Your school may be able to help you find a job. See if it has a career services department. It may offer workshops, résumé assistance, and help finding an internship, a part-time paid job while you're a student, and a job after college.

Look into a work-study program as well, where you work for pay in your chosen field and which is funded in part by the federal government. Eligibility is determined when applying for financial aid. If you qualify, your school should be able to help you find such a job.

For occasional money-making opportunities, there may be research on campus where you could be a paid test subject. Check the classified ads in your school paper or contact some of the individual schools. Medical schools are especially good places to look. Don't worry, you won't have to give up a kidney. Many such studies simply involve taking quizzes.

Another way to make some good part-time money is to become a tutor. You could work with high school students or even other college students.

A great online resource for finding a part-time job or an internship is LinkedIn. Search for "LinkedIn" and "student jobs." I'll talk more about using LinkedIn later in this chapter.

Working After College Graduation

Do you know what you want to do for a living when you get out of school? I'm sure you've either chosen a field or are thinking about one that you're interested in—one where you have some natural abilities and probably where you feel as though you can make a difference.

There's a cautionary tale about the work/meaning connection in the movie *About Schmidt*. In the opening scene, Warren Schmidt, played by Jack Nicholson, is staring at a clock on the wall of his office, counting down the minutes before his final day at work will be over and his retirement will begin. He has spent his career working as an actuary for an insurance company, where he rose to the position of assistant vice president.

At the end of his last day, Schmidt sits in the midst of his boxed belongings, watching the clock, waiting until 5:00 p.m., when the workday and his career will be over.

At a retirement dinner that evening, a longtime colleague toasts him, telling Schmidt he should feel "rich" to have devoted his life to something so meaningful. The look on Schmidt's face says he's not so sure. He once dreamed of having his own business but instead chose the security of a steady paycheck.

A Universal Longing

Shortly after Schmidt's retirement, his wife dies. The sudden changes—retirement, the loss of his wife of more than forty years—leave Schmidt wondering even more about the meaning of his life.

"I know we're all pretty small in the big scheme of things," he writes to Ndugu, a six-year-old Tanzanian orphan he sponsors in response to a television advertisement. "And I suppose the most you can hope for is to make some kind of difference, but what kind of difference have I made? What in the world is better because of me?"[2]

Our culture would have us believe that life is about competition. It tells us that happiness is found in having more than we have now and more than others have. But as Nicholson's character expresses so well, it's contribution that we long for, a sense that we're making a difference with our lives.

The Paths to Meaningful Work

I used to think there were just two types of jobs in the world: meaningful jobs and all the rest. Meaningful jobs were ones in which the work itself helped people or helped solve one of the world's great problems. Any other type of job was just a job. I now see it differently.

Some people do get the chance to do work that heals people, eradicates diseases, or other things that most would agree are inherently meaningful. However, there are many other types of jobs where great meaning can be found.

For some people, the satisfaction of providing for their family makes their work meaningful. For others, it's their relationships with coworkers that make their work fulfilling. For still others, their sense of meaning comes from how they use the fruits of their labor.

For example, I know a corporate attorney who doesn't find her day job to be all that meaningful. She's good at what she does and takes some enjoyment from using her skills to help her employer, but it isn't like she's changing the world through her work. To find the meaning she longs for, she lives far beneath her means in order to contribute significant time and money to a ministry dedicated to keeping kids out of gangs and helping homeless people get a new start. Doing so has helped her see her job as a means to a far greater end.

Maybe Meaning Is an Inside Job

When we struggle to find meaning in our work, one possible cause is that we think meaning is something our work should bring to us rather than what we bring to our work.

In his book *Authentic Happiness*, psychologist Martin Seligman tells a great story of a hospital orderly who meticulously selected pictures for the walls of a room where a close friend of Seligman's lay unconscious. The orderly explained, "I'm responsible for the health of all these patients. Take Mr. Miller here. He hasn't woken up since they brought him in, but when he does, I want to make sure he sees beautiful things right away."[3]

This orderly viewed his work as integral to the healing of patients. Another orderly might have considered this same work menial and meaningless. The first orderly saw his job as a calling; the second saw it as a source of income. The tasks are the same; only the perspective is different.

How do you see the career path you are pursuing? Will the work itself contribute to some greater good, or will your job be a means to some greater end?

Guaranteed Employment

In this day and age, there's no such thing as guaranteed employment. Not even close. However, there is a way to virtually guarantee your employability. That comes from how you approach your work.

Work diligently.
How would you work if you truly saw God as your boss? Would you come to your job on time? Would you put in the maximum amount of effort? You bet you would. You would do all you could to be great at what you do.

When we have the attitude that God is our boss, it doesn't matter what our job is or whether we think it is something we'll be doing only temporarily. We'll do it to the best of our ability. This was true of a guy I once knew who fell on hard times.

Everything about this guy said he came from wealth: his clothes, his way of speaking, his manners. Even though he came from money, he was out of money, so he started driving a cab. He decided he would be the most amazing cab driver his town had ever seen. He went to people's front door and carried their luggage to the cab. He held the door for them. He was endlessly courteous. He built a list of regular customers, and he made great money in tips.

On the other hand, we recently hired someone to do some work around our house—window washing, some painting. We'd hired the company before and were pleased with the quality of the work and the price charged. This time, though, was a different story.

The owner hired two college students to do most of the work. They completely missed a couple of windows, they dripped paint on our concrete porch, and they put the screens back into the window frames incorrectly. One screen fell from a second-floor window, hitting our backyard deck. I was just glad one of our kids wasn't out there at the time.

I will not hire that company again as long as those guys are working there. And I fear for their future. I'm sure that washing windows and painting are not their ideal jobs. But if you can't do the job in front of you well, how likely are you to do a different job better?

It's really another lesson taught by the parable of the talents, which we talked about in chapter 3. The two servants who made more of what had been entrusted to them were strongly affirmed and were then given more to manage. The same principle applies to how we steward our work abilities.

Those abilities go well beyond the actual skills needed for our job. In fact, technical skills are relatively easy to learn. What's harder to learn, and therefore more valuable, are the attitudes you bring to whatever work you do, starting with a hunger to keep learning.

Be a lifelong learner.

In most jobs, if we're standing still with our skill set, we're quickly falling behind. Things are just advancing too quickly:

technology, cultural trends, ideas. A key to keeping up is continuous learning.

After graduating, you might feel like you're done with school, but the people who excel in their work are the ones who never stop learning. Most large employers offer some form of tuition reimbursement, yet just 10 percent of eligible employees take advantage of that benefit.[4] That's valuable money being left on the table.

If tuition assistance is available to you at the job you take out of school, maximize that benefit. Find out what types of courses would be covered and go back to school. You'll learn more about your field while making important contacts among your classmates and teachers.

Even if your employer won't cover the cost of school, there are no- and low-cost ways to keep your skills sharp, such as the software training available from Lynda.com and the lectures on iTunes U (apple.com/education/itunes-u). Of course, you can check out the latest books in your field from the library, follow industry blogs, listen to audio books and podcasts, and more. Just reading the latest books and subscribing to the blogs of the leading thinkers in your field will give you a lead over others.

Find a great coach.

One trait that will help you connect with your teachers and your future employer is being teachable. I vividly remember a comment made by my boss at a golf course where I worked one summer: "I didn't start learning anything until I thought I knew it all."

He explained that when he was young, he thought he knew everything. He learned the hard way, by losing several jobs, that people don't really care for know-it-alls. It was humbling getting fired, especially more than once. And that humility served him well. When he became teachable, his next bosses valued him for that attitude.

Very often, successful people are more than willing to mentor younger people in their field. Even as you start your college career, it would be wise to seek out people who are working in the field you are pursuing. It might be family friends or people you know from church. Ask them if they would spend some time with you, sharing their stories of how they got to where they are and giving you advice about how you could best prepare for a career in that field.

Build a network.
One of the harshest lessons from the recession of 2008–2009 was just how fragile a job can be. Many thousands of people lost their jobs, and the average unemployed person stayed out of work for more than a year. A related lesson is the importance of continuous networking.

Online networking. If you haven't used LinkedIn (LinkedIn .com), set up an account, build your profile, and start building your network by inviting classmates, professors, and others you know who would be valuable business contacts to be part of your network.

Just remember, LinkedIn is much different than Facebook. LinkedIn is a professional network. Don't use it to tell your contacts about your weekend plans. Use it to build an online profile that describes your current status as a student, your field of study, and your future career plans. Companies often use LinkedIn to connect with students for internships and entry-level opportunities. There's even a student portal that you can find by searching for it.

Ask for recommendations as well. Even if you work a part-time job that's unrelated to your field, ask your supervisor for a recommendation that focuses on transferable job skills or work habits. What future employer wouldn't want someone who shows up on time, works well as part of a team, and goes the extra mile to do a great job?

Once you get out of school, if you need a contact at a company, you can look up that company and see if any of your contacts are connected with someone there. If so, you'll be able to see that connection. You can then ask your contact to make an introduction.

While you might think your degree and work experience are the only factors to consider when planning for your career, preparing for life after college has to do with more than your grades, your internships, and the part-time jobs you work while in school. It also has to do with your use of social media. Sure, you keep up with your friends on Facebook and other social media outlets. But did you know that prospective employers will most likely look at your Facebook page? Make sure there's nothing online that you wouldn't want an employer to see. Google yourself and see what comes up. Would you hire someone like you?

Offline networking. As you get closer to graduation, make the most of in-person networking opportunities. Networking has gotten something of a bad rap in recent years because it came to be seen as self-serving. People were encouraged to join organizations or go to events for the sole purpose of making connections. Today, networking events are more clearly promoted as such. If you're looking for work, there's nothing wrong with taking part in these events. Everyone knows why everyone else is there.

When you attend networking events, because you may be meeting a lot of people in a short amount of time, focus on collecting other people's business cards more than handing out your own. That enables you to control the follow-up process rather than waiting and hoping someone will contact you. Jot a reminder of what you talked about on the back of each person's card and send personalized follow-up notes.

Although many types of networking events can be helpful to your career, you will find it more enjoyable and effective to join clubs or other organizations you are genuinely interested in. You're more likely to make good contacts through your involvement in activities you care about than by joining groups for the sole purpose of networking.

Cast a wide net.
By some estimates, 80 percent of available jobs are not posted. They get filled through referrals. That's why having a great network is essential. Once you have a network of a hundred to two hundred people, it's amazing how easy it is to find someone who knows someone in a company where you'd like to work.

So build your network. You'll be able to see your connections' updates: promotions, new employers, and more. But stay in touch with some of your contacts via an occasional e-mail or phone call as well. Find out the latest. See if there are ways *you* could help *them*.

Be great at being yourself.
If two people have the exact same professional skills and experience, what's left to set one apart from the other? Interpersonal skills.

Communication skills (especially asking good questions and listening), relationship building, time management, and project management can help keep you in demand. All of these skills can be honed through the no- and low-cost options mentioned earlier.

Keep your career insurance in force.
With the uncertain nature of today's job market, it's the person who's been taking the above-mentioned steps who will succeed, either with his or her current employer or another one. It's like holding an insurance policy on one's career.

Of course, you could experience times of transition between employers, but those times will tend to be far shorter than average.

Memory Verse

Whatever you do, work at it with all your heart, as working for the Lord, not for men. (Colossians 3:23)

Reflection Question

1. Make a list of three to five people who are outstanding in the field you are pursuing and then think about these questions:

What makes them great? What skills do they have that set them apart? What personal character traits? What could you do to cultivate such skills and traits?

Action Step

Try to contact those three to five people who are outstanding in your chosen field and ask them for advice. Tell them how old you are and your future plans. See if they will give you some specific advice about how to succeed in the field.

Also, fill in the "Monthly Income" section of your *Cash Flow Plan*. Just estimate how much money is likely to flow into your life next month from a part-time job, your parents, or other sources.

Habit Four:
Giving Some Away

It is more blessed to give than to receive.

ACTS 20:35

I have found that among its other benefits, giving liberates the soul of the giver.

MAYA ANGELOU

It is completely appropriate to have some fun with money — to go on nice vacations, eat out, and enjoy the many other things money can buy, assuming you're not going into debt in the process. But when older people think back on their lives, it usually isn't the stuff they bought that gives them the most satisfaction. It's having the sense that they made a difference with their lives.

What difference would you like to make? What causes or issues do you care about? You can make that difference through your job, your family, your volunteer work, and other ways. But the best way you can make that difference is to regularly give some of the money you bring in to organizations that are working on the causes that matter to you. More specifically, the greatest satisfaction you will experience in your use of money will come from the investments you make in God's work.

Firstfruits Generosity

I made "Giving" the first outgo category on the *Cash Flow Plan* because God teaches us to make generosity our highest financial priority: "Honor the LORD with your wealth, with the *firstfruits* of all your crops" (Proverbs 3:9, emphasis added). *Firstfruits* means the first portion.

It isn't that God needs our money. He makes that abundantly clear in Psalm 50:12: "If I were hungry I would not tell you, for the world is mine, and all that is in it." In other words, God created and owns everything. He can make anything happen anytime. He isn't looking for a bailout or handout. Still, he teaches us to be generous. Here's why.

Designed to Be Generous

God is infinitely generous. He gave us our lives and the people in our lives. He gave us his Son. Because we were made in his image (see Genesis 1:27), that means that generosity is a central part of who we are. It's woven into the fabric of our souls.

When God blesses us financially, a central reason is so that we can be generous: "You will be made rich in every way so that you can be generous on every occasion" (2 Corinthians 9:11).

A Tangible Reminder of Our Highest Priority

The overall purpose of our lives is this: "Love the Lord your God with all your heart and with all your soul and with all your mind" (Matthew 22:37). What's one of the main roadblocks to living out that priority? According to God's Word, it's money.

Jesus said, "No one can serve two masters. Either he will hate the one and love the other, or he will be devoted to the one and despise the other. You cannot serve both God and Money" (6:24).

Isn't it interesting that Jesus chose money as the second "master"? He could have talked about the impossibility of serving God and our academic goals, or our hobbies, or any number of other things. It's true we are not to put any of those priorities above our relationship with Christ, but God identified money as his chief rival for our hearts.

When we give money to further God's work, we tangibly remind ourselves that he is our highest priority.

Amazing Returns on Investment

So what does it look like to give toward God's work? What *is* his work? And what sort of returns come from such investments? Let's take a look at three causes that God clearly cares about.

1. Spreading the gospel. Jesus said, "Go and make disciples of all nations, baptizing them in the name of the Father and of the

Son and of the Holy Spirit, and teaching them to obey everything I have commanded you" (Matthew 28:19-20).

In our household, when we receive our monthly investment account statements, some months our investment returns are up and other months they're down, but when we receive the monthly newsletters of missionary friends we support, the results are always up. Those newsletters are filled with stories of people who placed their faith in Christ as a result, at least in part, of the ministries in which we have invested.

Think about it: A financial investment in the spreading of the gospel is an investment that can help change a person's eternity.

2. Alleviating the suffering of the poor. You can't miss God's heart for the poor; it's written throughout the pages of Scripture. The Bible says, "He who is kind to the poor lends to the LORD, and he will reward him for what he has done" (Proverbs 19:17).

Earthquakes, hurricanes, plane crashes, and other disasters make news headlines around the world, as they should. However, there is a much larger disaster that occurs every day. According to the United Nations, an estimated 24,000 children die each day due to poverty, hunger, preventable diseases, illnesses, and other related causes.[1]

Think about it: A financial investment in the work of ministries that are serving the poor—helping to provide food, clean water, job training, medical care, and more—is an investment that can help save people's lives.

3. Supporting teachers of God's Word. There is no more important training we receive than instruction in God's Word, and we are called to help fund the work of those who do such teaching. The apostle Paul said, "Anyone who receives instruction in the word must share all good things with his instructor" (Galatians 6:6).

Think about it: A financial investment in the work of pastors who are teaching God's Word is an investment in people's (your own and other people's) growth in their relationships with Christ.

Let me say it again: By investing in God's purposes, we can actually help alter people's eternities, save people's lives, and further the teaching of God's Word. Those are pretty remarkable returns on investment, wouldn't you say?

The Personal Blessings of Generosity

Here's a final reason to make generosity our highest financial priority: The Bible promises that we will be blessed by living with a spirit of generosity.

At the beginning of this chapter, we read Proverbs 3:9: "Honor the LORD with your wealth, with the firstfruits of all your crops." Now let's read verse 10: "Then your barns will be filled to overflowing, and your vats will brim over with new wine."

Numerous other verses in the Old and New Testaments make the same fascinating, yet somewhat controversial, point. Consider:

> One man gives freely, yet gains even more; another withholds unduly, but comes to poverty. A generous man will prosper; he who refreshes others will himself be refreshed. (Proverbs 11:24-25)

"Bring the whole tithe into the storehouse, that there may be food in my house. Test me in this," says the LORD Almighty, "and see if I will not throw open the floodgates of heaven and pour out so much blessing that you will not have room enough for it." (Malachi 3:10; this is the only place in the Bible where God says to test him)

Give, and it will be given to you. A good measure, pressed down, shaken together and running over, will be poured into your lap. For with the measure you use, it will be measured to you. (Luke 6:38)

Remember this: Whoever sows sparingly will also reap sparingly, and whoever sows generously will also reap generously. (2 Corinthians 9:6)

This linkage between generosity and blessings is clear, yet it has become a bit trickier to teach about this aspect of generosity due to the spread of what's known as the prosperity gospel, which teaches a "give to get" approach to generosity.

Giving primarily out of a motivation to receive something back is surely an affront to God. As the apostle Paul asked, "Who has ever given to God, that God should repay him?" (Romans 11:35). God is the giver; we are the recipients of all he has generously given to us.

Still, there is an unmistakable promise seen throughout the pages of Scripture that blessings flow from generosity motivated by a grateful heart. Some people trace material blessings to their generosity. Others have experienced a closer relationship with God. In one form or another, blessings come from our generosity. It's how things work in God's economy.

Lisa's Story

Lisa once had nearly $10,000 of credit card debt. Soon after committing her life to Christ, she found herself feeling "convicted" to get out of debt, so she found ways to proactively manage her spending in order to free up extra money to put toward her debts.

During the process, she also wanted to begin tithing, so she made even more adjustments to her spending. She hoped to be able to increase her tithe a little at a time.

Then Lisa developed a third goal: to buy a new armoire! Her furniture was showing its age, and she wanted a nice armoire to hold her television and CDs. She even had a clear picture in mind of the perfect armoire, one with drawers to keep her CDs neatly stored away.

Shortly after starting to dream about a new armoire, Lisa learned that she was going to get a year-end bonus at work. The amount would enable her to buy just the armoire she wanted. She felt as though it were a reward for her commitment to get out of debt and start tithing.

But then she mentioned the bonus to a friend who had been walking with her in her new life of faith and in her journey toward getting out of debt. Her friend pointed out that the bonus money could pay off Lisa's remaining debts as well as be added to the amount she tithed. Lisa knew it was the right thing to do, but she was deeply discouraged about not being able to get her new armoire.

A week or so after paying off her final debt, she was taking the elevator in the building where she lived. Riding with her was a woman who was such a casual acquaintance that Lisa wasn't even sure she remembered her name correctly. In the course of the short ride to the second floor, the woman asked Lisa if she'd be interested in a free armoire. The woman explained that she had purchased a new television that didn't fit in her armoire. Stunned, Lisa went to see it and was even more surprised to see that it was exactly the type of armoire she had envisioned. Lisa said, "I felt as if God was telling me, 'I'm going to take care of you.'"

When we are generous, we live in concert with our design and we experience God's blessings. One blessing every generous person experiences is a greater sense of happiness. Even modern-day secular researchers studying the causes of human happiness have found a distinct link between generosity and happiness.[2]

How Much to Give

As a starting point, aim for giving away 10 percent of whatever money comes your way, such as money from your parents or from a part-time job. This percentage is what the Bible refers to as a tithe. The tithe was part of the Old Testament Law (see Leviticus 27:30), but it even transcended the Law, with the first example of someone giving 10 percent going all the way back to the first book of the Bible (see Genesis 14:20).

In the New Testament, it is clear that 10 percent is not the intended generosity stopping point. We read of Zacchaeus, who gave away half of what he owned (see Luke 19:1-10), and of

Paul's encouragement to "excel in this grace of giving" (2 Corinthians 8:7).

Where to Give

Look for trustworthy places to invest in the three priorities I mentioned earlier: bringing the gospel to those who don't know God, helping the poor, and supporting teachers of God's Word. Some pastors teach that all of a person's tithe should go to the church. They encourage supporting other Christian ministries but only with money above and beyond the tithe. If you are part of such a church, I encourage you to inquire about how your tithe may be used. You'll likely find that your church addresses each of the areas we've discussed.

In our family, a majority of our faith-based giving goes to our church because it's a one-stop shop for those three priorities. Our church helps reach the lost by supporting several missionaries and by preaching the gospel to those who come to our church for the first time. It also helps meet the needs of the poor in our community and in other parts of the world, and it is where we learn more of God's Word. However, we also give to other kingdom-centered organizations God has put on our hearts.

No matter what you discover about your church or the organizations or groups you consider supporting, pray about where God would like you to give. It may be to the church, elsewhere, or possibly a combination of the two, but making your decision with the leading of the Holy Spirit will ensure that your generosity is in line with God's will.

What About Donating to Museums and Other Nonprofits?

There are many great causes in the world, and I encourage you to support the nonprofits whose work you care about. However, if you are a Christian, the first priority for your generosity dollars is to support God's work in the world. Only these investments have the potential to generate eternity-shaping returns. Again, pray about where he would like you to invest.

How a Budget Helps

Jessica and Alex, who got married right out of college, agreed before getting married that they would tithe. But Alex candidly acknowledges it was a struggle to follow through. "I was getting my first salary, which wasn't a lot, but it was a lot more than I made when I was in school, so it seemed like a lot of money to give away."

The use of a budget helped. Once they plugged in all the numbers—designating 10 percent of their income for giving, covering their living expenses, and allocating some fun money for each of them—they were happily surprised to discover that they had a surplus of 3 percent. Jessica said, "The budget was the key. We never would have known we'd have extra. We felt as though we were poor and assumed it wouldn't work. If we didn't have a budget to show us that we were fine, giving 10 percent would have been tough."

How Can I Give When I'm in Debt?

Debt is one of the primary roadblocks to all of the good things money can do, including the ability to live generously. As we'll discuss later, the best way to speed up the process of getting out of debt is to pay more than the minimum due each month. The money you are giving away each month can look like an easy source of those additional funds. However, before tapping that money, here are three recommendations.

1. Pray for discernment. God knows your situation, so ask him what you should do. I know people who have taken this step who have sensed God telling them to give at least at the 10 percent level while getting out of debt, even though it would take them longer to get out of debt. So that's what they did, trusting that God had a purpose in mind that could be accomplished only through an extended time of debt repayment.

2. Rethink other budget categories first. Because of the high value God places on generosity, before deciding to give less than a tithe, consider other ways to free up money for accelerated debt repayment, even extreme ways. How about cutting out cable TV while getting out of debt or even going without an Internet connection? How about getting rid of your car? How about going on a temporary entertainment-spending fast, seeking out all of the free things to do in your area?

3. Always give a choice gift. If you sense God's freedom to give less than a tithe for a season, at the very least keep in mind the biblical standard of a firstfruits gift. That's a first priority, or a choice gift.

Think back to the story of Cain and Abel, Adam and Eve's sons. When they both brought offerings to the Lord, Cain brought "some of the fruits of the soil," which scholars have explained means that he gave a portion of his crops but not the best portion. By contrast, Abel brought "fat portions from some of the first-born of his flock." In other words, he gave a choice gift. "The LORD looked with favor on Abel and his offering, but on Cain and his offering he did not look with favor" (Genesis 4:3-5).

The Great Financial Paradox

Our culture advises, "Pay yourself first." It makes intuitive sense, doesn't it? If we are to experience financial success, our first financial priority must be to set aside a portion of all that we earn for savings or investing. Yet money is a struggle for so many people.

God's solution is the counterintuitive teaching, "Pay your purpose first." Because the overarching purpose of our lives is to love God, the most tangible way we can fulfill that purpose financially is to make the support of his work in the world our highest financial priority. Go ahead and put such teaching to the test. You'll soon discover the blessings that flow from living the generous life you were designed to live.

Memory Verse

It is more blessed to give than to receive. (Acts 20:35)

Reflection Questions

1. How do you feel about giving 10 percent of all the money you receive to God's work in the world? If you're hesitant about that idea, why?
2. What's your reaction to the idea that your generosity dollars could actually alter a person's eternity, save a person's life, and further the teaching of God's Word?

Action Step

Take a look at your monthly income on your *Cash Flow Plan*. Now fill in the "Now" and "Goal" spaces in the "Giving" section. Set a goal in faith of giving 10 percent of all the money that comes into your life each month.

Habit Five:
Putting Some Away

In the house of the wise are stores of choice food and oil, but a foolish man devours all he has.

PROVERBS 21:20

I have enough money to last me the rest of my life, unless I buy something.

JACKIE MASON

I still remember the first time it happened. I was leading a workshop for Christian college students, and one of the students asked me whether putting money into a savings account reflected a lack of faith. I was so surprised by the question that I had to make sure I had heard it correctly. And then it happened again. Just a few months later, while teaching another group of Christian college students, someone asked the same question.

I have to say, I love the question. It reflects a heart that is oriented around fully trusting in God. I point out that God encourages us to maintain a reserve. Just look at the verse at the beginning of this chapter where the Bible says it's "foolish" to use up all that we have. I also point out, though, that there's a second reference to savings in the Bible where God warns against the foolishness of saving too much. Let's read Luke 12:16-21:

> The ground of a certain rich man produced a good crop. He thought to himself, "What shall I do? I have no place to store my crops."
>
> Then he said, "This is what I'll do. I will tear down my barns and build bigger ones, and there I will store all my grain and my goods. And I'll say to myself, 'You have plenty of good things laid up for many years. Take life easy; eat, drink and be merry.'"
>
> But God said to him, "You fool! This very night your life will be demanded from you. Then who will get what you have prepared for yourself?"
>
> This is how it will be with anyone who stores up things for himself but is not rich toward God.

So we're foolish if we don't save anything and we're foolish if we save too much.

The line between wise saving and foolish hoarding is not clearly marked. One thing is certain, though: It is not drawn with numbers but with the attitude of our hearts. As we save for future goals, we would be wise to regularly ask ourselves whether our faith is truly centered on God or on the size of our savings and investment accounts.

Savings Defined

Saving and investing money are two different things. Money that you put into savings is primarily for three purposes: emergencies, bills or expenses that occur at some point each year but not every month, and things you want to buy or expenses you're going to have within the next one to five years.

Money that you invest is for longer-term goals, such as buying a house or, as abstract as this probably seems right now, paying for your retirement. We'll look at investing in chapter 10. In this chapter, our focus will be on saving.

Save Like Crazy

Here's my recommended ideal plan for building savings. For every dollar you bring in while you're in school, put forty cents into savings. What? That's insane, right? I know, I know. It sounds like a ton of money, and I'm sure you can come up with plenty of other more enjoyable uses for that money.

The thing is, though, by the time you graduate, you're going to need some money. Some *serious* money. You'll need to make a deposit on an apartment, some new clothes for work, maybe a car. Plus, you'll need some money in reserve for all the bank account–draining stuff that seems to go wrong in life.

So if you have any discretionary money coming in each month, get in the habit of saving a healthy portion of it—ideally, 40 percent.

Different Types of Savings

I recommend that you have a checking account and three separate savings accounts: one for an emergency fund, one for periodic bills or expenses (those that you know you're going to have at some point during the year but not each month), and one for things you want or will need to buy within the next five years.

To keep things easy, you'll probably want to use one bank or credit union for these accounts. Doing so will simplify your life in that you can check your balances online at just one site.

Some online banks allow you to set up one savings account but split it up into sub-accounts that are designated for different purposes. These accounts should truly be *savings* accounts. Don't mingle this money with the funds you keep in a checking account.

Checking Account. If you don't have a checking account yet, look for one with a low minimum-balance requirement. Before signing up, be sure to understand any fees the bank or credit union charges. Some financial institutions offer checking accounts specifically designed for students. Be sure to explore online banks as well. You might also want to wait until your student orientation session before choosing where to open an account, as financial institutions are often represented at such events and sometimes offer sign-up bonuses. Again, be wary of any fees. Ask specifically what fees are involved now and what fees may be charged down the road.

Savings Account Number One: An Emergency Fund. One of the few certainties in life is that you will experience your share of financial emergencies. I'm not talking about that last-minute invitation to the social event of the year for which you absolutely *need* some new clothes. That money should come out of your clothing budget. I'm talking about unexpected and big medical expenses that aren't covered by insurance, as one example. Or losing your $300 chemistry textbook.

You probably won't need a ton of money in an emergency fund while you're in college, but building the habit of maintaining an emergency fund will serve you well after college when you *will* need to keep more money in reserve. When you start working full-time, the worst financial emergency you could experience is the loss of your income, whether through unemployment, illness, or injury. Having money in savings is an essential key to surviving such an emergency without having to take on debt.

Plus, having some money in reserve is a great way to minimize stress. Not long ago, I worked with the market research firm Synovate to conduct a national survey, asking people how much financial stress they were experiencing. I also asked whether they pay their credit card balances in full each month, whether they use a household budget, and whether they have money set aside for emergencies.

All three habits are important. However, financial stress was most closely correlated with how much money people had in reserve. Those who had no emergency fund or considered their credit cards to be their emergency fund were the most stressed. Those who were the least stressed had a healthy emergency fund.[1]

Aim for building an emergency fund with a balance of $1,000. When you get out of school, you'll want to keep stocking that emergency fund.

I used to think three to six months' worth of savings constituted a sufficient emergency fund for someone in the working world, but during the most recent recession, I saw with fresh eyes just how bad things could get. Unemployment was high and people who lost their jobs were remaining out of work for a long time. That's why the new normal for an emergency fund for someone who is out of school and working full-time is a minimum of six months' worth of living expenses.

Savings Account Number Two: Short-Term Financial Goals. Once you have your emergency fund sufficiently stocked, open a short-term goals savings account and start stocking it with the 40 percent of income you had been using to build your emergency fund.

This savings account is for relatively big-ticket expenditures you anticipate having to make, such as a car or other post-college start-up expenses. It would be ideal to graduate with $5,000 in such an account.

Try not to touch your emergency fund or this short-term financial goals savings account while you're in college. If you have to tap your emergency fund, temporarily stop adding to your short-term goals account and use the money that was going into that account to replenish your emergency fund. Once it's back up to the proper level, go back to adding to your short-term goals savings account.

Savings Account Number Three: Periodic Bills and Expenses. If you own a car, which I don't recommend until you're out of school, you will have a vehicle-insurance bill. If that bill is due every six months and you haven't been saving for it, where will you get the money? For all such bills and expenses, estimate the total annual cost, divide by twelve, and put that amount into a separate savings account each month. Gifts can be another example of a periodic expense since so much of a typical person's gift budget is spent in December. Figure out an annual gift budget and put one-twelfth of that amount into this separate savings account each month.

Money for this savings account does not come from the 40 percent of income that I want you to allocate to savings. It comes from the budgeted amounts you have for gifts, insurance, vehicle maintenance, and other periodic bills or expenses. You simply take the total of all of those monthly amounts and automatically transfer it to this savings account each month. Then, when you need to spend the money, you transfer it back to your checking account.

Where to Put Your Savings

You typically won't earn much interest on savings, but that's okay. With money you save, you mostly just want the money to be there when you need it.

Some good choices about where to put emergency-fund money include a bank (traditional or online), credit union savings, or money market account. Online banks often pay higher interest rates than traditional banks.

Make It Automatic

One of the best ways to build savings is to have a preset amount of money automatically transferred from your checking account to savings each month. This option works best if you have consistent amounts of money automatically coming in each month. If not, you may need to make this transfer into savings manually. To remember to do that, put a recurring reminder in your electronic calendar, scheduling a savings deposit on the first of every month, for example.

Overdraft Protection

As I mentioned earlier, be careful to understand any fees charged by the bank or credit union you choose. One fee in particular to watch out for is an overdraft-protection fee. *Overdraft protection* is a confusing term. Protection sounds like a good thing, but in this case it isn't.

Depending on your bank or credit union, overdraft protection usually kicks in when you try to buy something or pay a bill using your checking account and you don't have enough money in the account to cover the cost. It also may go into effect if you try to make an ATM withdrawal and you don't have a sufficient balance.

If you have chosen to have overdraft protection on your account, your bank or credit union will approve the transaction and then smack you with a fee as high as $34. If you don't have overdraft protection, your transaction will be denied and you will not incur a fee. In effect, overdraft protection gives you the freedom to spend more than what's in your checking account in exchange for a fee. Not a good idea.

Banks and credit unions are required to ask their customers whether they want to opt in for overdraft protection. Previously, many financial institutions simply let people overspend their accounts and then hit them with a fee. It became a very lucrative source of revenue.

The best alternative to overdraft protection is knowledge: Know how much money is in your account and don't spend more than that. If you insist on having overdraft protection, do you have a savings account at the same bank or credit union where you have your checking account? If so, you may be able to link the two accounts, automatically drawing funds from your savings account to cover any overspending you may do with your checking account. In some cases, there is no fee for such a service. Or, if there is a fee, it will typically be less than the traditional overdraft-protection fee.

Bottom line? Your finances will be better protected if you keep close tabs on your checking account balance and opt out of overdraft protection. By doing so, you will be opting in for over-*spending* protection.

Memory Verse

In the house of the wise are stores of choice food and oil, but a foolish man devours all he has. (Proverbs 21:20)

Reflection Questions

1. Do you tend to save too little or too much? Why?
2. Where would you draw the line between wise saving and foolish hoarding?

Action Step

In the "Savings" section of your *Cash Flow Plan*, write in an amount equal to 40 percent of your income (the money you earn or receive from your parents or other sources each month), or whatever stretch-goal amount you can commit to. Then, if you don't have a savings account, open at least two: one for an emergency fund and one for periodic bills and expenses. Once you have an adequate emergency fund, open a third savings account for short-term goals.

Habit Six:
Avoiding the Big D

The rich rule over the poor, and the borrower is servant to the lender.

PROVERBS 22:7

Debt — noun. An ingenious substitute for the chain and whip of the slave driver.

THE DEVIL'S DICTIONARY

Going into debt is a blast. I know all about that. If a credit card company deems you worthy of its card, you'll be able to buy all kinds of stuff you can't afford: trips, clothes, restaurant meals. Living beyond your means is great fun—until it isn't anymore and your debt load starts to feel like a wheelbarrow full of bricks that you're pushing up a mountain.

That's when you discover that getting out of debt is way, way tougher than getting into debt. I know all about that. It took me four and a half years to pay off my $20,000 of credit card debt. Four and a half long years of sending $500 per month, each and every month, to my creditors to pay for restaurant meals I ate long ago, trips I took long ago, and clothes I no longer wore.

"Not Much"

I once heard someone in her early twenties say she had $6,000 of credit card debt. She literally shrugged her shoulders at the amount and casually described it as "not much."

Not much? Well, think about this. Let's say that by some miracle she stops going any further into debt. And let's say she regularly makes the minimum monthly payments required by the credit card company. Using some common assumptions about interest rates and minimum-required payments, it's going to take her more than forty-two years to pay off that "not much" level of debt, and she's going to pay over $16,000 in interest along the way!

If you're going to be successful with money, you absolutely need to commit to getting out of debt as soon as you can and then staying out of debt. The only exception is a reasonable mortgage, but that's probably not your focus right now.

If you're going to get out of debt and stay out of debt, you're going to need some passion behind that commitment because walking around carrying a big load of debt is so common that it feels normal.

But it's not normal. It's crazy. It will keep you from achieving your goals, mess up your most important relationships, and stress you out.

Do the uncommon thing. Live with a ruthless passion for avoiding debt and you will be well on your way to achieving an uncommonly good financial life.

Student Loans

Are you planning to use one or more student loans to pay for college? It's a pretty common part of the college experience. About 75 percent of students graduate from college with student loan debt.

I realize you may not think you have any choice over the matter. You may think you won't be able to afford college without a student loan. But I'd like to challenge you on that. At the very least, I'd like you to clearly see what you're getting yourself into.

The average debt load of college students who graduate with student loan debt is over $25,000. That's such a big number that it can seem like funny money, but there's nothing funny about lugging around that much debt.

Assuming an interest rate of 5 percent and a payoff period of ten years, a $25,000 loan works out to a monthly payment of $265. That's a lot of money for anyone, and especially for someone just starting their career. With average salaries among new grads at $30,000, that loan payment amounts to over 10 percent of your $2,500 in monthly gross income.

Take a look at the Recommended Spending Guide in the appendix (see page 178). The guide is based on a single person making $30,000 with no debt—no car loan, no credit card balances being carried from month to month, no loans from mom and dad, and no student loans. So you'll have to come up with that

$265 by spending less in other categories. Trust me, it won't be easy.

Your "Housing" category is probably your best bet for finding extra funds to pay down debt. If you moved back home with your parents after college, you should pay them something, but you probably won't have to pay $625 per month. Or maybe you could afford an apartment if you had a roommate — or two or three.

If you're figuring on a different amount of student loan debt, you'll find a calculator on the government's student aid website at studentaid.ed.gov. Run some numbers and see what your monthly payment is likely to be.

As a side note, use student loans only for educational expenses. Some students treat the loans as part of their entertainment budget. Spending ten years paying off your tuition and room-and-board expenses is bad enough, but paying for pizza over the next ten years is just plain crazy.

Rules of Thumb Could Be Your Ruin

You'll probably run into advice from various "experts" who say you should keep your student loan payments to 6 to 8 percent of your income. You can easily get the impression that it'll all work out. But the fact is, it *isn't* working out for a lot of people.

According to recent figures, one out of every four borrowers with outstanding student loans has a past-due balance. You don't want to get behind in your student loan payments. For government-backed student loans, Uncle Sam will get paid one way or another.

Miss a payment on a federal student loan and your wages

could be garnished. And no, "garnish" in this case does not refer to a piece of fruit or parsley that restaurants put on your plate. It refers to money being automatically, legally ripped out of your paycheck and rerouted to your student loan provider before you receive your check. The government can even snag your federal tax refund.

I don't mean to be all gloom and doom. I just want you to see that your student loan is going to end up costing you a big chunk of money every month for a long time. Do all you can to avoid this type of debt.

Avoiding Student Loans

One option, which is very common in other countries, is to take a gap year. Don't go to college right away. Take a year after high school and work to earn money for college. This can also be a great option if you don't know what you really want to do with your life. College is a very expensive place to try to figure it out.

There are entire books devoted to the topic of getting through college without student loans, but another of the most common ideas is to spend two years at a community college. Of course, make sure your credits will transfer to the four-year school you plan to attend. Assuming they will, it'll cost you far less in tuition, and if you can live at home, you'll save on room and board.

Also, make sure you finish school on time. Plenty of students fail to graduate in four years. Plan your classes with the help of an academic advisor, who should be able to help you choose a path that leads toward graduation in four years.

If a Student Loan Is Inevitable

If it's truly impossible to avoid a student loan, you need to plan ahead for the day when you'll have to start making payments on that loan.

Once you graduate, you'll probably have six months before you'll need to start making payments. A crucial first step is to build your future monthly payment into your budget right away. If you take on all sorts of bills and expenses that use up all of your income right away, how will you ever work the student loan payments into your budget when you need to start making those payments?

Use the calculator I mentioned before (studentaid.ed.gov) to estimate your monthly payments, and then start making those payments right away. Put the money in a bank or credit union savings account. That'll get you used to making the payments, and it'll give you a nice head start on paying off your student loans early.

When your first payment is due, send it plus all the money you've been accumulating in the savings account. Be sure to also let the company servicing your student loan know your current address. A lot of people applying for a mortgage get turned down because they've missed some student loan payments. They didn't notify the company servicing their student loan of their change of address and missed the notification that their loan payments were due.

Pay More Than the Minimum

The amount of your student loan can be so high that it's hard to even get your mind wrapped around being free of such debt. A lot of students decide to live with their loans — to put up with them for as long as the *normal* payoff time frame runs, usually ten years.

Lugging a student loan around for ten years may be normal in the sense that lots of people do it, but if you want to experience uncommon financial success, you need to think of ten years of student loan payments as very far from normal.

There's never a prepayment penalty with student loans, so get on the fast track toward ditching that debt. Find some money in your budget to pay extra. Seeing how much more quickly you'll be out of debt can be a great motivator. Use the Accelerated Debt Payoff Calculator in the resources section of SoundMindInvesting.com to run some what-if scenarios: What if you put an extra ten dollars toward your student loan payment each month? What if you came up with an extra fifty dollars?

Look into Creative Repayment Options

If you have to take out a student loan, there are a number of programs available that may help you repay your loans.

Public Service Loan Forgiveness. If you work in a public service job, you may be eligible to have a portion of your student loan debt forgiven. Such jobs include working for a local, state, or federal government agency; a tax-exempt nonprofit organization; the military; education; law enforcement; and more. You have to pay on your loans for ten years, but your loans would typically be structured as twenty-five-year loans. In that case, fifteen years' worth of payments could be forgiven. There's more information about the program at studentaid.ed.gov.

National Health Service Corps. If you study to become a doctor, dentist, or other healthcare professional, you may be able to have your student loans repaid by working in a community in need. Find out more at nhsc.hrsa.gov.

Federal Student Loan Repayment Program. The federal government has a program in which agencies are allowed to use loan repayment as an employee recruitment or retention tool. Agencies, at their discretion, are authorized to repay up to $10,000 per year per employee up to a maximum benefit of $60,000. For more information, go to the U.S. Office of Personnel Management website at opm.gov and search for "student loan repayment program."

How to Use Credit Cards

There are some personal-finance writers who say no one should have a credit card. I'm not one of them. I believe most people can learn to use credit cards wisely. Here are four essential rules for doing so.

First, only spend preplanned, budgeted amounts with your credit cards. Let's say you have a budget that allows you to spend $50 on clothing every month. You can charge $50 worth of clothing each month.

Second, track your credit card spending. This is something very few people do. What usually happens is a person gets his or her credit card bill and immediately assumes there's been a mistake. They're absolutely certain they didn't spend as much as the statement says.

As they prepare to call customer service, they start going through the charges one at a time to find the error, but to their amazement, there are no errors. They really *did* spend all that money.

Overspending with credit cards is easy because handing over that piece of plastic just doesn't seem very real. Cash is real. It feels real when you give the money to the cashier, and there's a certain reality to looking at an empty wallet once you've spent all your cash.

Not so with credit cards. Paying with plastic seems abstract. There's a lot of research showing that people tend to spend more when using credit cards. They supersize their fast-food meals, leave bigger tips, and generally spend more loosely when paying with plastic. Plus, you never get the feeling you're out of money when you use credit cards. It isn't like the plastic shrinks the more you use it.

That's why you have to know how much you can afford to spend (step 1), and it's why you have to record how much you spend with your credit cards as you make each purchase (step 2).

If you use an electronic money-tracking tool, such as Mint .com, it'll record your spending for you. If you don't use such a tool, you could use an Excel spreadsheet or a simple paper-and-pencil money-tracking tool, such as the *Cash Flow Tracker* I introduced in chapter 4.

If you have a budget that allows you to spend $60 on entertainment each month and you use your credit card to buy movie tickets for $20, you need to write that down. That way, the next time you plan a night out, you can see that you have $40 left in your entertainment budget for the month.

Third, pay your balance in full each month. One of the worst possible money moves you can make is to carry a balance on your credit cards. Once you start carrying a balance on a credit card, that's a tough habit to break, and you'll waste a ton of money on interest payments. Never, ever carry a balance on a credit card from month to month.

Fourth, if you can't follow the first three steps, don't use credit cards.

How to Get Out of Financial Jail

If you have a credit card with a balance that you're carrying from month to month—and plenty of college students do—make it one of your highest priorities to get out of that debt as soon as possible. Here's how.

First, just say no to taking on any more debt. Mark this day as the day you decide to go no further into debt. Take your credit cards out of your wallet or purse. Keep them somewhere safe, but keep them out of reach. Do whatever it takes to make it as tough as possible to take on any more debt.

Second, tell someone else about your "no more debt" decision. Contact a close friend or family member. Let him or her know how much debt you have, explain that you're committed to ditching that debt once and for all, and ask for support in your pursuit of that goal. Ask the person not to beat you up about your debt but to simply ask you from time to time how the process is going.

Telling someone else about your debt will likely be a life-changing conversation. It's uncommon behavior to talk to people about money in our culture, and it's especially uncommon to tell someone about our financial *problems*. However, having someone else know about your debt will be absolutely one of the most helpful steps you can take to get out of debt. And here's what else might happen. If you work up the courage to tell someone else about your debt, don't be surprised if he or she ends up telling you about theirs.

Debt is so common that there's a good chance the person you choose as an accountability partner will have debt as well. If he or she is willing to come clean with you, you could be each other's accountability and encouragement partners.

So, who will you tell? Stop reading right now and contact that person. Make the call. Send the text. Do it now. Why wait?

Third, fix your payments. Here's one of the most important things you need to know about how credit card debt works. Let's say you have a $1,000 balance on a credit card and you stop going any further into debt. And let's say you pay the minimum amount that the credit card company requires each month. If you do that, your required monthly payment will actually *decrease* a little bit each month. This month, it may be $20. Next month, it might be $19.90, and then $19.80, and on and on.

Isn't that incredibly kind of your credit card company? I mean, who else that you owe money to asks for less each month? Of course, it isn't kindness at all. It's math. Your monthly payment is based on a percentage of your balance, usually between 2 and 4 percent. If your balance is going down a little each month, then your required payment will go down a little each month too. Paying this declining minimum payment each month is what will keep you in debt for approximately . . . forever!

In this case, trying to pay off of credit card debt by taking the declining-minimum-payment route, it could easily take you more than twelve years to pay off that debt, and it could cost you nearly $1,400 in interest. Charge $1,000 worth of stuff. Pay $2,400 for it. Uh, no. Not a good idea.

Here's a better idea. *Fix* your payments. If you can afford $20 this month, you can afford $20 next month. Paying this fixed amount will get you out of debt way faster. By fixing your payments at $20 per month, you'll go from a payoff plan of twelve years down to a plan of less than eight years. Just by continuing to pay the amount you paid last month, you'll wipe out more than four years of credit card payments.

One of the reasons it's so easy to fall for the old declining-minimum-payment trick is that the minimum-required payment goes down by such a small amount each month. It's easy to miss the fact that it went down.

So, write down this month's required minimum. Then, next month, when your credit card company showers you with kindness and asks for a little less, tell them, "Thank you very much for your generous offer, but I'd like to be out of debt before I have grand-kids, so I'm sending you what I sent you last month."

Of course, you don't need to include a note. Just send them the money—at the very least, the same amount you sent them last month.

Fourth, pay more than the fixed minimum. If you can find a little extra money to put toward your debts each month—an extra ten or twenty dollars—that'll really get you moving toward becoming debt-free. In our $1,000 balance example, if you paid $30 each month, you'd be out of debt in about four years. Make that $40 a month, and you'd be out of debt in about two and a half years.

You can see how much faster various accelerator amounts will get you out of debt by using the Accelerated Debt Payoff Calculator in the resources section of SoundMindInvesting.com. At the very least, fix your payments. But if you can put a bit more toward your debts than the fixed minimum, that's even better.

What About Vehicle Loans?

Here's a quiz. Which would you rather have? A four-year-old BMW 325 or an eleven-year-old Honda Civic? Let's say you could drive away from the dealership with either one for five thousand dollars. Simple choice, right? You're going with the BMW.

Ah, but you're on to me. You know it's a trick question. Here's the catch. With the Honda, you would own it outright. It costs $5,000. That's it. But with the BMW, the $5,000 is just a down payment. It also comes with a $12,500 loan. With the BMW, you'll need to pay about $250 per month for five years. The $250 per month may even fit within your current budget. If you purchased the Honda, though, you could save or invest that $250 each month.

Let's take a look at what happens with your money depending on which option you choose. After five years, if you had chosen the BMW, you would have spent $20,000, including about $2,500 in interest you *paid*. With the Honda, you would have spent $5,000. And, if you had saved or invested the $250 (the money you're not putting toward a monthly car payment) in a way that earned 3 percent interest, you'd have more than $16,000, including about $1,000 in interest you *earned*.

That's a lot of money we're talking about, whether you buy a car outright or finance one through a loan. And think about how much more you could save or invest if you don't buy a car at all!

Even if you do have the money to purchase a car outright, think about the expenses involved in maintaining and running it. Cars eat. They eat gasoline, insurance, maintenance, repairs, license fees, parking tickets, and more.

My best recommendation for you: If you have a vehicle right now while you're in college, get rid of it. Unless you absolutely need it, you'd be better off going through college without a car. Let someone else on your dorm floor be the cool kid who has a car. Hitch rides from him or her. Sure, chip in some gas money, but hold off on buying your own car as long as you can. That'll give you the freedom to start saving and investing.

In our culture, having lots of debt is so common that it feels normal, expected, even unavoidable. My encouragement to you is to do the uncommon thing: Avoid debt with a passion. It will seem odd to be the one without all those monthly payments, but you'll get used to it.

Memory Verse

The rich rule over the poor, and the borrower is servant to the lender. (Proverbs 22:7)

Reflection Question

1. Before reading this chapter, were you planning to take out a student loan? If so, what are some steps you could take to avoid borrowing money to pay for school?

Action Step

If it's going to be absolutely necessary to borrow money for college, use the calculator at studentaid.ed.gov to estimate your monthly payments so that you're prepared for what you'll face when you get out of school.

Habit Seven:
Managing Your Number

A good name is more desirable than great riches; to be esteemed is better than silver or gold.

PROVERBS 22:1

It takes many good deeds to build a good reputation, and only one bad one to lose it.

BENJAMIN FRANKLIN

Financially, your reputation boils down to a three-digit number: your credit score. It doesn't matter what people *say* about how responsible you are with money; what matters is how responsible you *actually are*, especially in managing your use of credit. Each credit-related action you take is recorded on your credit report, tallied, and turned into your credit score.

A good credit report and score will help you get the best rate on a mortgage and a lot more. Insurers, cell phone service providers, and a growing list of other companies base their decisions about working with you and at what rates, in part, on your credit report and score. More and more landlords and employers are checking the same information before renting you a place to live or hiring you.

Here's what you need to know about credit reports and credit scores.

How to Establish Credit

It's helpful to have a credit profile before leaving college, but you won't have one until you start using credit. Using a debit card won't help because it isn't a line of credit. What you buy with a debit card comes directly out of your checking account.

Still, getting a credit card isn't so easy for a young person. The Credit Card Act, signed into law in 2010, has made it more challenging. You can't get your own credit card if you are under twenty-one unless you have a co-signer or you can prove that you have enough income to pay your bills.

Dangers of Co-Signing

When someone co-signs for someone else's loan, they are taking responsibility for that loan. If the person they are co-signing for doesn't make the required payments on the loan, the co-signer has the legal obligation to pay. If you co-sign for a loan for someone who ends up filing for bankruptcy, that person may be protected from attempts to collect on the loan, but you will not be protected. No wonder the Bible warns against co-signing for someone else's loan: "Don't agree to guarantee another person's debt or put up security for someone else" (Proverbs 22:26, NLT). Also see Proverbs 6:1-5; 11:15; 17:18.

Bottom line? Don't ask someone to co-sign for you and don't co-sign for someone else's loan. This even goes for family members. Having to make good on a loan that a family member can't afford can harm your relationship with that person. If you really want to help a family member with a purchase, consider giving the person the money with no expectation of repayment.

Where to Apply If You Have a Job

If you have a part-time job, you may be able to get a card in your own name. Still, you may find it difficult to get a Visa, MasterCard, or American Express card. It can be easier to get a retail or gas station card. After you've been using such a card for six months or so, try applying for one of the big three. Or if you have a checking account and debit card at a bank or credit union, try applying for a credit card there.

If none of those options works, you might want to apply for what's called a secured card at your bank or credit union. With a secured card, you put some money into a savings account and the card is issued for the amount you have in savings. In essence, you are *securing* the credit limit with the money you have on deposit. Before going this route, though, find out whether the bank or credit union reports information about its secured-card users to the credit bureaus. If not, a secured card won't help you establish a credit score.

Another Option

Another way to start building a credit score is for you to become an authorized user on one of your parents' credit cards. This is different than having them co-sign for you. It's *their* line of credit, not yours. They are simply giving you access to their account. Your parents will be able to monitor your use of the card and you'll start establishing a credit profile, "piggybacking" off your parents' profile. (Note: Make sure your parents are responsible users of credit or you'll get the *negative* halo effect of their mistakes!)

How to Build and Maintain a Good Credit Score

Once you have a card, start using it, but use it only for pre-planned, budgeted items as described in chapter 8, and be sure to pay the entire balance each time you get a statement. If you find yourself starting to carry a balance from month to month, stop using the card. It would be better to graduate without a credit history than to graduate with the habit of carrying a balance on your credit cards.

Credit scores range from 300 to 850. Unlike cholesterol, the higher the number the better. The best rates on mortgages, for example, go to people who have a credit score in the mid 700s or higher. The credit bureaus use five factors to determine your score.

1. Payment History

Thirty-five percent of your credit score is based on your track record of paying your bills on time. Do all that you can to pay your bills by their due date. Here's your guide to building an impenetrable late-fee-avoidance system.

Pay right away. Do you have a stack of bills sitting on your desk? Are they at least stacked with the one that needs to be paid the soonest on top? Even so, to avoid late fees, get in the habit of paying your bills the day they arrive. Sure, you'll lose "the float," the time between the arrival of the bill and the due date, where your money could be sitting in your interest-bearing checking account racking up all that .01 percent interest. But getting slammed with a late fee, typically between $25 and $39, will wipe out about thirteen lifetimes of earnings at that rate.

Pay online. If you're still paying bills by check, consider switching to electronic payments, which arrive faster and never get lost in the mail. The most surefire way to avoid late fees is to automate your bill payments. Just about any monthly bill can be paid automatically. Whether you should do so is partly a matter of whether you trust that the right amount will be billed each month.

We pay our mortgage, health insurance, and some of our utilities automatically. However, we take a manual approach to paying our phone and credit card bills online, preferring to check those bills more closely for accuracy before clicking the "pay" button.

Ask for reminders. No matter how you pay, sign up for e-mail or text reminders about upcoming bills. Most companies that you spend money with on a regular basis offer electronic reminders. Because we use Mint.com to manage our household budget, which also sends notifications of upcoming bill due dates, we get two electronic reminders for most of our bills.

Remind yourself. One of the reasons air travel is so safe these days is because of redundant systems. If one flight-control computer system fails, there's another one to automatically take its place. You can build redundancy into your on-time bill-pay system as well by putting reminders in your calendar. Most electronic calendars allow you to set up recurring events.

If one of your credit card bills is due on the eleventh of every month, you can set a reminder one time and have it show up on your calendar every month on the same day. Of course, set the reminder for at least a few days *before* the due date to make sure the bill gets paid on time.

I use iCal on my Mac. To set a recurring reminder, just choose "new event" from the File menu, and under "repeat," choose "monthly." If you're using Google Calendar, hit "create," add an event, click the "repeat" box, and fill in the details.

I also use different colors for different activities in my electronic calendar, which makes the bill due dates really stand out.

And remember, it isn't just credit card companies that dole out late fees. Insurance companies, libraries, video-rental companies, and many others will slap you with a fee if you pay your bill late or return their stuff late. So put *all* of your due dates in your calendar.

If somehow a bill slips through your impenetrable late-fee-avoidance system and you incur a late fee, call the company that hit you with the penalty and plead for forgiveness. If you've been a customer for a while and have had a clean record up to now, you stand a good chance of getting the fee wiped off your bill. However, if at first you don't succeed, ask to speak to a customer-service supervisor. Be super kind, accept responsibility, and let them know what steps you've taken to avoid paying late ever again (see above steps).

2. How Much Credit You Use

Thirty percent of your credit score is based on how much of your available credit you use. This is what the credit bureaus refer to as credit utilization. Using 30 percent of your available credit or less is good; 10 percent or less is ideal. So if you have a credit card with a $1,000 credit limit, try to charge no more than $100 each month.

This aspect of building a strong credit score can be somewhat confusing. I'm not talking about carrying a balance of $100. Some people believe you have to carry a balance on your credit cards in order to build a credit score. You do not. I never want you to carry a balance. I'm simply talking about using your credit card to buy $100 or less each month. You see, the credit bureaus just take a look at how much you have charged on your card at a certain point in time each month. They won't tell you when.

3. How Long You've Been Using Credit

Fifteen percent of your credit score is determined by how long you have used credit. There isn't much you can do about this one other than to start using credit. Over time, this part of the credit-score equation will work more and more in your favor.

I'm often asked in workshops whether to close old, unused accounts. This is generally not a good idea, but not because doing so will erase your credit history. Even if you closed an account, positive information about the account would stay on your report for ten years, negative information for seven years.

The problem with closing an old account has to do with credit utilization. Closing an account lowers your total available credit, which may increase your utilization, and that can lower your credit score.

4. How Many New Accounts You've Opened Recently

The amount of credit you have applied for recently impacts 10 percent of your score. Opening new credit card accounts as you make your way through the mall in order to get all those 10 percent discounts on your purchases tends to discount your credit score.

5. Your Use of Various Types of Credit

Your mix of installment loans, revolving credit, and a mortgage is an important part of the final 10 percent of your score. Having some of each type of credit is ideal, at least from the credit bureaus' perspective. Installment loans are those with a fixed payoff period, such as a vehicle or student loan. Revolving loans are open-ended loans, such as credit cards. However, I don't recommend taking on new loans just for the purpose of trying to improve your credit score.

Understanding Your Credit Report

Everyone is entitled to one free report each year from each of the three credit bureaus: Experian, Equifax, and TransUnion. Get your reports at AnnualCreditReport.com. Here's what to look for in each of their major sections.

Credit Summary. Toward the top of your Equifax report, under "Accounts," you will see your credit utilization, or what it calls "Debt to Credit Ratio." This is the area where you can do something to impact your score the most in the least amount of time.

If you have a high debt-to-credit ratio, you will raise your score if you can pay down your debt, especially credit card debt. The improvement should show up within thirty days.

Account Information. Are there any accounts you don't recognize? This could be a sign of identity theft. If you see such accounts, contact those creditors directly and let them know that the accounts are not yours.

Also, under account information, check to see if there are any accounts listed as open that are actually closed. Review your credit limits and compare them to the limits stated on your credit card statements. If the report lists your credit limits as being lower than they really are, your credit utilization will be incorrectly high.

Check to see if there are any late payments noted. For Experian, you want your open-account status listed as "Open/ Never Late." For Equifax, "Pays as Agreed." For Transunion, "Paid or Paying as Agreed." If any accounts are listed otherwise and you believe you have never been late with a payment, contact the creditor. Even if you don't have proof that you paid on time, let them know that you believe a mistake has been made and ask if they will change it on your credit file.

Inquiries. An inquiry occurs anytime anyone checks your credit report. A "hard inquiry" occurs when you apply for credit and the prospective lender checks your credit report or score. Lots of recent hard inquiries will work against you.

"Soft inquiries" come from lenders looking to make you a preapproved credit offer, existing creditors reviewing your file, prospective employers and insurers, or yourself when you check your own report. These do not hurt your credit score.

Personal information. Check to see that the following information is correct: the spelling of your name, your birth date, your current and previous addresses, your Social Security number, and current and past employer information.

If you see any problems on your report, file a dispute. Instructions are on your report. Make copies of forms you fill out and any responses you get. The bureaus must investigate your dispute within thirty days unless they deem it to be frivolous.

How to Guard Against Identity Theft

The single best step you can take to guard against identity theft is to zealously guard your Social Security number. If someone steals your credit card number, they can run up charges on your account, but chances are good that the credit card company won't make you pay. On the other hand, if someone gets your Social Security number, they can open new accounts in your name, which you may not discover for months or even years.

Only a handful of organizations have a legitimate need to know your number. They include your employer, your bank and brokerage house, and your doctor. If someone else asks you for your Social Security number, double-check with his or her supervisor to see if it is really necessary. You may need to talk with *that person's* supervisor. A cell phone service provider told one person I know that a Social Security number was required. It took talking with eight different people to find out that a driver's license number could be used instead.

It may be a hassle to avoid giving out your Social Security number, but it's worth it. Undoing the damage caused by identity theft, according to the Federal Trade Commission, costs victims an average of sixty hours and nearly $1,200.

If you ever become a victim of identity theft, the Federal Trade Commission offers guidance on its website at ftc.gov.

Do the Right Thing

Credit scores have an aura of mystery. There's no end to the articles offering this strategy or that for increasing your score. The truth is, there are two very basic steps everyone can take to build and maintain a good score: Pay your bills on time and use a relatively small amount of your available credit. Focusing on those two things will go a long way toward keeping your financial reputation—your credit score—strong.

Memory Verse

A good name is more desirable than great riches; to be esteemed is better than silver or gold. (Proverbs 22:1)

Reflection Questions

1. If applying for a credit card required you to go before a judge and present evidence that you are ready for the responsibility, what evidence would you present?
2. If someone who knew all about you was also in court to argue against the wisdom of granting you credit, would they have any evidence to make their case? What would you say in your defense?

Action Step

Go to AnnualCreditReport.com and try to pull your reports. That will tell you whether you have any. If so, follow the advice in this chapter on how to review your reports. If not, take the steps I've outlined to establish a credit profile.

If you have a credit report, purchase your credit score for $19.95 by going to MyFico.com. You'll have your choice of purchasing your TransUnion FICO score or your Equifax FICO score. For now, it doesn't matter which one you choose; just buy one. I know it seems unfair to have to pay for your own score, but that's just the way it is. It's important that you know your score so that you can see the impact of being proactive in managing it.

10

Habit Eight:
Playing Great Offense

He who gathers money little by little makes it grow.

PROVERBS 13:11

I am opposed to millionaires, but it would be dangerous to offer me the position.

MARK TWAIN

I'm going to take a wild guess that you spend approximately zero minutes each week thinking about retirement. Retirement is something old people think about, and you are far from old.

The problem is that by the time you're old, it's too late to start thinking about retirement. If you spend your life spending all that you make, it'll be pretty much impossible to save enough to be able to retire. You'll have to keep on working or move in with your adult children, or both.

You, on the other hand, are in a very different position. Retirement may be this fuzzy concept set somewhere in the very distant future, but if I can get you thinking about it now, it'll serve you amazingly well. That's because, as I said in the first chapter, your age is a huge plus in building wealth through investing. Huge.

The Financial Fan

This is a good time to introduce a concept I call the financial fan. The more common name for it is compound interest. When it's working for you, it's like having a stiff financial wind at your back; it's one of the best deals going. When it's working against you, it's like having a brutal financial wind howling in your face. The beneficial type of compound interest is the type associated with saving and investing. The negative type is the interest charged by creditors.

We've already looked at a couple of examples of the bad type. Think about the woman who had $6,000 of credit card debt, which she described as "not much." Do you remember how long it would take her to pay off that debt if she made the minimum-required payments each month? More than forty-two years! That's what happens when you get compound interest working *against* you.

Now let's see what happens when you get compound interest working *for* you. When you earn interest on money you put into savings or an investment, that interest earns interest, and then that interest earns interest, and on and on. Interest earning interest is what's meant by *compound* interest.

The Power of Momentum

Compound interest doesn't have much of an impact in the beginning of a long-term investing program, but eventually it does. Consider this. Let's say you put $100 a month into an investment and earn an average of 8 percent interest per year. After the first year, you'll have invested $1,200. That's $100 per month for twelve months. And because you earned 8 percent, you'll have earned $45 in interest by the end of that first year.

Now let's check in at the ten-year mark. At that point, you will have put in $12,000, but it will be worth nearly $18,300. Not bad.

But look at what happens after twenty years. If you've been faithful at investing $100 each month over that time, you will have put in $24,000. And if you've been able to earn 8 percent per year, your $24,000 will have turned into $58,900. Wow. Now you've earned more in interest than you've contributed. But let's keep going.

Let's say you stick with this for forty-five years. You will have invested $54,000. That's $100 per month for forty-five years. Again, assuming an average return of 8 percent per year, your $54,000 will have turned into more than $527,000! Isn't that amazing? Now, that's some financial wind in your sails. That's the power of compound interest. No wonder one of the world's smartest scientists, Albert Einstein, called compound interest "the eighth wonder of the world."

You Have Time on Your Side

Let me say it again: Your key advantage is time. Think about this. Imagine being forty years old. You're married. You have a couple of kids and a mortgage. You realize you haven't been putting any money away for retirement, so you really need to get started.

You punch some numbers into an online calculator and are stunned at what you find out. The calculator tells you that you're going to need to have at least $1 million saved by the time you're sixty-five. In order to hit that goal, you'll need to start socking away more than $1,000 each month. But the roof has been leaking and you need to start thinking about college for the kids. Where are you possibly going to come up with that kind of money?

But you're not forty. You're just about to start college. In order to achieve the same goal—a million dollars by the time you're sixty-five—you need to put away *just* $135 each month.

I know, that still sounds like a lot of money. After all, your main job right now is going to school and no one's paying you for that. But if you have any money coming in, if you can put aside a little bit of it now, you'll be able to avoid that heart-stopping, wallet-draining experience the forty-year-old had.

Even if you have to wait until you start your first full-time job, that's okay, but the sooner you start the better.

If you earn $25,000 a year in your first job, putting 10 percent into your employer's retirement plan should be plenty. Assuming a 3 percent salary raise each year and an 8 percent return on your money, you'll hit age sixty-five with more than $1.3 million in retirement savings. And that's assuming your employer doesn't provide a match. But plenty of employers do match some of the money you set aside for retirement. For every dollar you put into the retirement plan, they'll put in fifty cents or even a dollar. Of course, that will leave you with even more.

A Little Now Beats More Later

When Frank and Sandy were twenty-five years old, they scraped together $200 per month and invested that money in a way that generated an average annual return of 8 percent. However, when they turned thirty-five, they had to start helping their elderly parents and could no longer make those investments. Because they didn't need to touch the money they had invested, they left it where it could continue earning 8 percent per year. When they turned seventy, their $24,000 ($2,400 invested each year for ten years) had grown to $600,000.

Let's compare them to their friends Joe and Karen. When they were twenty-five years old, they found it impossible to come up with any money to invest. They had trips to take, furniture to buy. But they figured that they were young and that there would be plenty of time to save for retirement later. They decided to begin investing when they turned thirty-five and invested $200 per month until they were seventy years old, along the way earning 8 percent each year. After thirty-five years of investing $200 per month — a total of $84,000 — their nest egg totaled just $462,000. They invested *more than three times* as much as Frank and Sandy had yet ended up with nearly $140,000 less.

As these stories show, when you're young is when you stand to gain the most from the power of compound interest. Make it a priority to begin investing a portion of all you earn early in your life and you will likely end up in your later years with a nest egg that can generate enough interest to live on comfortably. The important point is to get started with investing as soon as you can.

Of course, there's no guarantee what your rate of return will be. Investing comes with the risk of loss. And one of the results of the recession that started in 2008 is that a lot of young people have become scared of the stock market. In fact, a survey of Generation Y investors, people ages eighteen to thirty, conducted by the mutual fund company MFS Investment Management, found 40 percent agreeing with this statement: "I will never feel comfortable investing in the stock market."[1]

That's too bad because one of the riskiest things a young person can do with investing is play it too safe. If you put money only into a bank savings account, there's no way the interest will amount to very much. A bank savings account is a great place for an emergency fund, but it's a lousy place to save for a long-term goal such as retirement.

At your stage of life, you have time to ride out the ups and downs of the stock market, and there will be some of both. But history has shown that the stock market is one of the best places to generate good long-term investment returns.

The Most Important Key to Investing Success

Do you know what separates the great investors from the lousy ones? Do the greats just have a knack for picking winning stocks?

Do they have access to information that mere mortal investors don't?

Actually, the most important key to investing success is much more boring-sounding. It's making sure you choose the right asset allocation.

What in the world is that? I'm glad you asked. It's how you spread your investment dollars across various types of investments. For example, if you have $1,000 to invest, choosing whether to put it all into a stock-based mutual fund or half in a stock fund and the other half in a bond fund is asset allocation.

As hard as this may be to believe, choosing the right asset allocation is even more important to your investing success than which specific investments you choose.

What's the Right Allocation for You?

So how do you decide on the right asset allocation? There are people who have devoted their careers to answering that question and you can get their recommendations for free. The investment research organization Morningstar has come up with what it calls Lifetime Allocation Indexes. It has three different recommended asset allocations for someone nineteen years old: aggressive, moderate, and conservative. If you're in your teens or twenties, my recommendation is to go with their aggressive allocation. But it's not worth losing sleep over. If you're more comfortable with the moderate allocation, that's fine. At your age, though, the conservative allocation is too conservative.

Allocation Chart

	Aggressive	Moderate	Conservative
Stocks	**93%**	**89%**	**81%**
U.S.	56%	53%	49%
Non-U.S.	37%	36%	32%
Bonds	**3%**	**7%**	**15%**
U.S.	2%	5%	11%
Non-U.S.	1%	2%	5%
Inflation Hedge	**4%**	**4%**	**4%**
Cash	**0%**	**0%**	**0%**

Let's define these terms and make some sense of the chart. First of all, a stock represents ownership in a company. If you buy a share of IBM stock, you become a part owner of IBM. If the company does well, the stock should rise in value. If not, it may fall. You can buy stock in U.S.-based companies or those based elsewhere, hence the distinction between U.S. stocks and non-U.S. stocks.

Bonds are "debt investments." Think of it this way: When you invest in a bond, you are loaning money, usually to a city or company. When a city issues bonds (municipal bonds), it is typically trying to raise money for a project such as putting in a new sewer system. When a company issues bonds (corporate bonds), it is usually trying to raise money for expansion or some other business purpose.

The city or corporation agrees to pay interest on the bonds they issue, and as long as they don't get into financial trouble, you should get the interest they agree to pay. Just as there are U.S. and non-U.S. stocks, there are U.S. and non-U.S. bonds.

For inflation hedges, commodities include gold, silver, and other precious metals. They are thought of as inflation hedges because as inflation goes up, they usually go up in value as well.

Cash typically refers to money market funds, a very conservative type of investment.

Even with its moderate asset allocation, Morningstar is recommending a pretty aggressive investment approach for nineteen-year-olds: mostly stocks, a bit of bonds, and some inflation hedge–type investments. It's understandable that they would choose an aggressive mix. It's a standard bit of thinking in the investment world, which I agree with, that the younger you are, the more risk you can afford to take.

A sixty-year-old wouldn't want any part of this asset allocation because she doesn't have the time to ride out the stock market's ups and downs. She's going to want a much more conservative mix. At this stage of life, she doesn't have enough time to ride out some stock market downturns.

How to Keep It Simple

Already, this may be sounding kind of complicated. After all, in order to implement Morningstar's recommendation, you now have to choose specific stocks, bonds, and commodities. Here are two ways to add a lot of simplification to this process.

First, invest in mutual funds. A mutual fund is a pool of money from lots of investors. Either a professional mutual fund manager is making the decisions as to which stocks or bonds to buy, or the mutual fund is designed to mirror an index.

For example, maybe you've heard of the S&P 500. It's an index that represents the stocks of five hundred of the most widely held publicly traded companies whose stocks are available through U.S. stock exchanges. The index is considered a good gauge of the overall U.S. stock market. You can buy mutual funds from numerous mutual fund companies that are set up to mirror indexes such as the S&P 500. No investment manager is researching what stocks to buy or sell. The fund owns stock from each of those five hundred companies.

Investing in mutual funds is typically less risky than investing in individual stocks because of the fact that mutual funds are inherently diversified. Each one may hold hundreds of different stocks, bonds, or other investments.

However, if you were going to implement Morningstar's recommended asset allocation using mutual funds, you'd still have some work ahead. You'd need to choose a U.S. stock fund, a non-U.S. stock fund, a U.S. bond fund, a non-U.S. bond fund, and a fund that invests in commodities. And there are plenty of funds to choose from in each category.

One Really Simple Solution

Fortunately, you can invest in a single mutual fund that is set up to provide you with your ideal asset allocation. And even better than that, this single mutual fund will change its asset allocation automatically as you get older, becoming more and more conservative, as it should.

This type of mutual fund is called a target-date fund. The

target date refers to the year of your intended retirement. Most of the big brokerage houses offer such funds: Fidelity, T. Rowe Price, Charles Schwab, Vanguard, and others. You just choose the fund that has the year of your intended retirement as part of its name, and you'll know that it is set up with an asset allocation the company believes is right for you.

Keep in mind that target-date funds don't all use the same asset allocation, even with the same type of investor in mind. Some are more aggressive than others. Morningstar, which doesn't sell investments (so it has no reason to be biased), recommends the target-date funds of Vanguard and T. Rowe Price.

Two other factors are important in choosing a target-date or other type of mutual fund as well. The first is its expenses. Each mutual fund charges management fees. Because Vanguard has some of the lowest fees in the mutual fund industry, it would be a good choice, especially since Morningstar singled it out for having what it believes is a particularly good approach to asset allocation.

The other factor, which may be especially important to you, is the minimum amount needed to invest in such funds. As I wrote this book, Vanguard required a minimum initial investment of $1,000. When making future investments, if you do so by check, it needed to be for at least $100. However, if you set up an automatic monthly investment, there was no minimum for future investments. You could add as little as $1 per month.

T. Rowe Price required a minimum initial investment of $2,500, or $1,000 if you invested in the fund through an IRA (more on that in a minute). Each additional investment needed to be for at least $50.

If you have less than these minimums, Fidelity may be a good choice. While it required $2,500 as an initial investment in its target-date funds, if you invested through an IRA, you could get started with just $200 as long as you committed to an automatic deposit of $200 each month.

Charles Schwab offered the lowest minimum-required initial investment I could find: just $100 to get started and $1 for additional investments.

The organization I work for, Sound Mind Investing, also offers investment solutions, ranging from "Just the Basics" for those who want to keep things simple to a "Fund Upgrading" strategy for those who like to take a more hands-on approach. You can learn more at SoundMindInvesting.com.

By now, some people reading this book have a thick glaze covering their eyes. I know that for a lot of people, investing is not the most interesting topic in the world. But hopefully the idea of having $1 million to your name *is* exciting, so it's important to know about the things I'm covering here and start investing as soon as you've built your savings accounts.

Before you do, though, there's one final thing you should know about investing: the benefits of doing so through an IRA.

Keeping Uncle Sam Out of Your Pocket

In this investing section, so far we've covered the importance of starting to invest as soon as possible so you can tap into the amazing power of compound interest. We've talked about the importance of asset allocation, noting that the easiest way to get the proper allocation is to invest in a good target-date fund.

Now we come to the final section in our chapter on investing.

If you have earned income—money you *earn* as opposed to money given to you by your parents, for example—I recommend that you invest for your later years with a Roth IRA. A Roth IRA is not an investment; it's a vehicle through which you make investments.

Mutual funds and stocks are investments. But if you invest in either one *through* a Roth IRA, you'll get some important tax benefits. Although there's no immediate tax break on the money you put in (it doesn't lower your taxable income), you get some nice tax benefits from that point forward. You don't pay taxes on any money you earn (capital gains taxes), and you don't pay taxes on the money once you start taking it out in your retirement (income taxes).

Maybe you're concerned about not being able to touch that money until you're old and gray. While it's true that it's best to go into a Roth IRA with the mindset that you won't, in fact, touch it until you're old and gray, a Roth comes with some flexibility built in. You can withdraw the money you put into it at any time. You can't take *earnings* out without a penalty, but you can take out the money you put in.

Where to Open a Roth IRA

You can open a Roth IRA with $1,000 at Vanguard. At Fidelity, you can open an IRA with just $200, but you'll have to continue contributing $200 every month. At Charles Schwab, you can open an account with no initial deposit as long as you automatically deposit $100 per month.

Investing Summary

This has been a long section, I realize, but it's really important to know some of the essentials about investing and to get in the game as early as you can. If I were in your shoes, I'd get an emergency fund and other savings accounts built as soon as possible. Then I'd start investing with a Roth IRA.

Memory Verse

He who gathers money little by little makes it grow. (Proverbs 13:11)

Reflection Questions

1. Are you ready to begin investing? In order to answer yes, you should be using a *Cash Flow Plan*, have no credit card or vehicle debt, and have a solid base of savings.
2. Are you drawn to a more active investing style in which you figure out the right asset allocation for you and then choose your own mutual funds, or are you drawn to a simpler approach such as investing in a target-date fund? Why?

Action Step

If you have your savings accounts adequately built, fill in the "Investing" section of your *Cash Flow Plan*. A Roth IRA is not an investment. It's a vehicle through which you make investments. Start investing by using the full amount you had been putting into savings each month: 40 percent of your income (the money you earn or receive from your parents or other sources each month), or whatever stretch-goal amount you had been putting into savings.

11

Habit Nine:
Playing Great Defense

The prudent see danger and take refuge, but the simple keep going and suffer for it.

PROVERBS 27:12

There are worse things in life than death. Have you ever spent an evening with an insurance salesman?

WOODY ALLEN

If you ever have trouble sleeping at night, just pick up an insurance contract and start reading. You'll be out in no time.

Few topics—financial or otherwise—are more boring than insurance, yet it's important to fight the yawns, learn what you need to know, and make sure you have the right coverage. Otherwise, an uncovered illness or injury could saddle you (or your parents) with so much debt that you'll need to drop out of college. Plus, many schools require you to have health insurance before they'll allow you to enroll.

Here are the three main types of insurance that are likely to be relevant to you. Talk these topics over with your parents since they may still be footing the bill. Don't assume they've got it covered.

Health Insurance

Up to this point in your life, you've probably given little thought to health insurance. When you got sick, you went to the doctor. Somehow the bills got paid. That "somehow" was very likely a combination of your parents' health insurance and your parents' checking account.

As you head off to college, the best option for health insurance is very likely the one you already have: your parents' health insurance plan. Assuming you don't have a job that provides health insurance, you should be able to remain on your parents' plan.

This is usually the best option because it's typically the most comprehensive coverage you can get and you can't be excluded from coverage or charged more if you have a preexisting condition. Ask your parents to double-check with their employer's human resources department to make sure you can stay on their plan.

Also, ask them to find out about the rules and regulations for in-network coverage. That relates to which doctors are members of an organization willing to accept negotiated rates with the insurance company. If you go to school a long distance from home, doctors in that area might not work with that particular insurance company, which means you may end up paying more for out-of-network doctors' visits. One solution is to schedule annual physicals for when you are home, but you can't schedule all possible medical needs for those times.

If the town where you're going to college has no doctors who accept your parents' health insurance, see if out-of-network providers are covered by the insurance plan to some degree. That would be better than nothing. Also, if you need specialized care, see if a doctor in the town where you go to school can make the referral or if you'll need a referral from a hometown doctor. Also, if you are covered under your parents' dental plan, find out whether you can see a dentist in the town where your school is located.

If your parents don't have employer-provided health insurance, see what sort of health insurance your school offers and at what cost. Typically, you'll find that school health insurance plans are not all that generous, setting fairly low limits on how much they'll pay for specific conditions or your total annual healthcare costs. Some may not cover you for preexisting conditions or they may charge more for such coverage.

A final option is an individual health insurance plan. There are websites such as eHealthInsurance.com that can help you find an individual policy. You may find that you can get better coverage this way than through your school's plan, with higher coverage limits and wider access to doctors. You'll have to weigh the benefits against the costs. Student loan provider Sallie Mae

(SallieMae.com) also offers student health insurance and various other types of insurance.

Of course, one of the best steps you can take to minimize the cost of healthcare is to take care of yourself. Get some exercise on a regular basis. Chances are that your school has a gym where you can work out for free. Also, eat healthfully and do something most college kids don't do: get enough sleep.

Property Insurance

Think about the stuff you plan to bring to college. Laptop computer? Digital camera or camcorder? Stereo? Television? DVD player? Sports gear? Gaming system? What would happen if you lost any of that stuff or if it got stolen?

Your least expensive option is to have your parents check with the agent responsible for their homeowners policy to see if your items are covered as well. Be sure to ask about coverage for any especially expensive items. Your parents may need to add a rider to their policy. And what about all those expensive textbooks? Would they be covered if you lost one?

CSI (CollegeStudentInsurance.com) and National Student Services, Inc. (nssi.com) are two companies that specialize in property insurance for college students. Even if you'd be covered by your parents' homeowners policy, it may be worth it to get a quote from these companies. You (or your parents) may find that you can get better coverage than your parents' homeowners policy at a reasonable price and with a lower deductible.

Take an inventory of the stuff you plan to take to school.

Capture it with a camcorder and then keep the memory card in a safe place. The Insurance Information Institute also has free software (KnowYourStuff.org) and a free smartphone app that makes this easier. You may also want to engrave especially expensive items with your name and phone number.

Vehicle Insurance

As I mentioned in an earlier chapter, I strongly recommend that you not own a car while you're in college. If you do, though, you'll need to carry vehicle insurance.

One of the main ways to save on the cost of vehicle insurance is to opt for higher deductibles. If you have a claim, that's the amount that you would have to pay before your insurance coverage would kick in. With a $500 deductible, for example, if you damaged your car, you'd have to pay the first $500 of the cost of getting it repaired. Your insurance would then cover the rest.

Vehicle insurance policies typically have two deductibles: one for collision and one for what's called comprehensive. Collision is for what it sounds like: damage to your vehicle if you are in an accident. Comprehensive covers such things as vehicle fire, vandalism, and theft.

The key here is realizing that you are on the hook for the amount of the deductible if you have a claim. So before considering a higher deductible, make sure you have enough money in savings to cover the deductible amounts. Also, make sure you're comfortable knowing you'd be responsible for those amounts should you need to file a claim.

At a certain point, you may want to drop collision or comprehensive coverage altogether, keeping only liability coverage, which will pay for damage you cause to someone else's vehicle or for their medical expenses.

Some Insurance You Probably Don't Need

Tuition Insurance. Offered through schools by third-party insurers, these policies refund a portion or all of the cost of tuition and on-campus housing if you leave school early. Reasons for leaving typically must be because of medical or mental health reasons or the death of an immediate family member.

One reason you can probably go without this coverage is that many schools will refund all of the tuition cost if you withdraw by a certain deadline, usually within the first few weeks of a new semester. In some cases, schools will refund a prorated amount after the deadline.

But talk it over with your parents. If it buys them some peace of mind, maybe tuition insurance will be worth it to them.

Life Insurance. There's almost no reason for you to have life insurance until someone is dependent on your income, such as when you get married and especially when you have kids.

For now, the main reason why you *might* need life insurance is if you have a *private* school loan and if a parent or someone else is a co-signer on the loan. Remember, though, that having a co-signer is something I don't recommend.

With federal government–backed student loans, if you die (fun topic, right?), the loan is forgiven. The same *may* be true with some private loans, but not always, so if you have a private student loan, check its provisions. You or your parents may want to take out a life insurance policy on you. That way, if something happened to you, your parents' grief wouldn't be compounded by the aggravation of having to continue making payments on that loan. The life insurance proceeds would pay it off.

Insurance is one of those things people don't like to deal with but are glad to have when they need it. Take the time to go over your insurance coverage with your parents before heading off to college. It will give you and your parents some added peace of mind.

Memory Verse

The prudent see danger and take refuge, but the simple keep going and suffer for it. (Proverbs 27:12)

Reflection Questions

1. Some people think that taking out insurance policies reflects a lack of faith in God's provision and protection. What do you think?
2. Where would you draw the line between being a good steward by carrying adequate insurance protection and going overboard with too much insurance protection?

12

Habit Ten:
Spending Smart

If you have not been trustworthy in handling worldly wealth, who will trust you with true riches?

LUKE 16:11

Economy is half the battle of life; it is not so hard to earn money as to spend it well.

C. H. SPURGEON

If you're going to do all that we've already talked about — give some money away, put some away, ruthlessly avoid debt, and patiently pursue interest — you're going to have to be really smart about how you spend.

This isn't about frugality. With apologies to those who do frugal well, I've never cared for the term. For me, it's always conjured up images of Dumpster diving, refusing to tip any more than 15 percent, and making all spending choices based on what's the absolute cheapest option. Okay, I'm exaggerating, but not by much. Mostly, I've thought of frugality as not much fun, where the overarching principle is to spend as little as possible. Who wants to live that way?

Repositioning Frugality

A better financial path begins with a better term, and the one I prefer is *money smart.* To be money smart is to know how to get great stuff at great prices, all the while realizing that the cheapest option may not actually be the most cost-effective one.

Being money smart also means being really good at making trade-offs, happily choosing to spend less in one category in order to spend more on something else that's more important.

If you want to take a great trip for spring break, being proactive about how much you spend on clothing or entertainment leading up to the trip won't feel like suffering. It will feel smart because you're doing all you can to save for something that matters more: the trip.

When you're money smart, you rarely, if ever, have to pay full price.

Getting Your Biggest Expense Right

I'm sure you don't have a mortgage yet, but eventually you will. When you're ready to buy a condo or house, the ideal is to keep your monthly housing costs to no more than 25 percent of your monthly gross income. And when I say housing costs, I'm talking about the combination of your mortgage, property taxes, and homeowners insurance.

That's a helpful benchmark for renting as well. Most new college grads rent an apartment after graduating, unless they do a stint back at Mom and Dad's place for a while. If and when you go looking for an apartment, choose one that requires no more than 25 percent of your gross monthly income, including renters insurance. In fact, if you really want to prepare for home ownership, include utilities in that 25 percent as well.

Because housing is typically a person's largest expense, it's really important to get this decision right. For a lot of people, their home owns them. They buy or rent such an expensive place that they can't afford to save or give anything away each month. That's no way to live.

Utilities

One way you can save on the cost of utilities is by switching from regular lightbulbs to LED or compact fluorescent lightbulbs. These bulbs cost more than regular bulbs, but they use a fraction of the energy and last much longer.

The only caution is that compact fluorescent lightbulbs (CFLs) contain a small amount of mercury. If you break one, you have to be careful about how you clean up the mess. When one burns out, do not put the bulb in your regular garbage; take it to a hazardous-waste disposal facility. Some retail stores—including Home Depot, Lowe's, and Ikea—are drop-off sites for CFLs. (For more on how to clean up a broken CFL and where to find a disposal facility, go to earth911.com.)

Transportation

Our home may be our castle, but for many people, their car is an extension of themselves. According to a study cited by Juliet Schor in her book *The Overspent American*, nearly half of all car owners see their car as a reflection of who they are.[1]

The belief that we are what we drive (coupled with the auto industry's heavy use of planned obsolescence) often leaves us on the vehicle-financing treadmill. We tend to build short-term relationships with our vehicles and long-term relationships with our vehicles' loan officers.

A better approach to buying cars is to build long-term relationships with our vehicles and send our vehicles' loan officers packing. In fact, as you'll see in the Recommended Spending Guide (see page 178), which is designed for use when you're out of college, not having a vehicle payment is an essential part of building a financial life that works.

As I said before, I recommend not having a car while you're in college. If you can avoid owning a car until you're out of school, that will help you build savings. How will you get home for visits? Many colleges offer discounts on bus or train tickets.

Once you're ready to buy a vehicle, plan to keep your car for at least ten years, preferably longer. The financial freedom that brings is far more beneficial than the short-lived thrill of driving a car with temperature-controlled cup holders. Here are some guidelines for how to own a car.

1. Buy, don't lease. Although you may pay less each month for a leased car than you do for a car you buy and finance, you won't own anything at the end of the lease. You'll just have to start making payments on another vehicle. In order to have the margin to be generous, save, and invest, it helps a lot to have no monthly car payment.

2. If you end up financing a vehicle loan (please, do all you can to avoid this!), keep making those payments even after your vehicle is paid off. Just send them to a savings account instead of your lender. If you can afford the payment today, you can afford it once the loan is paid off.

Then keep that vehicle for at least another five years, and when it's ready to be replaced, you should have plenty of money to buy your next one with cash.

3. It's usually best to buy a well-maintained used car, but not always. Vehicles used by dealers for test-drives or loaners will be less expensive than a brand-new car. But vehicles that are one to two years old are where the real deals can be found; they often cost 30 to 40 percent less than the original price.

Still, I've loosened up on this one a little bit in recent years. If you're paying cash, planning to keep your vehicle for ten years or more, and don't opt for all the high-margin extras, buying new *may* make sense. You just have to compare the cost of a new car with a used car and factor in other benefits, such as the warranty.

4. When deciding which car to buy, choose one known for

reliability. *Consumer Reports* lists its picks for the best used vehicles by price on its site for free.

5. Consider all of the costs. Some cars are more expensive than others to insure and maintain. When the exhaust system goes out on a dual-exhaust car, for example, it's going to cost a lot more than it would on a car with a single-exhaust system.

Edmunds.com has a helpful True Cost to Own calculator that enables you to compare vehicles based on the costs of fuel, insurance, maintenance, replacement parts, and depreciation. As a point of comparison to what the Edmunds website tells you, call your insurance agent to get quotes on a few cars you're considering. You can run a separate fuel-economy comparison at Fueleconomy.gov.

6. Be sure to budget some money for maintenance. One of the biggest mistakes car owners make is not budgeting for this category. The first problem with not planning for maintenance expenses is that you might not keep up with basic maintenance. With no money budgeted for oil changes, you'll let it go — until you hear a strange banging noise coming from under the hood. What I've discovered is that the louder the bang, the bigger the bill.

The second problem is that when unavoidable major expenses come up, you'll have to go into debt to pay the bill.

The amount to budget for maintenance and repairs depends on the age and condition of your vehicle, but a good ballpark is $75 per month per vehicle.

With vehicle maintenance, there are plenty of months when we don't spend anywhere close to $75. But throw in the need for new tires every five or six years, the occasional major tune-up, and replacing the side mirror that we scraped off backing out of our own driveway and $900 per year comes out about right.

There are certainly no moral prohibitions against heated seats or headlight wipers. However, moving through life without the ball and chain of a vehicle payment shackled to your leg will go a long way toward helping you live with financial freedom. Your car may not be able to parallel park itself, but you'll get over that.

Textbooks

If you've never purchased a textbook before, you're in for a shock. They're really expensive. Here are some ways to save.

Contact your professors and ask for an advance copy of the list of required books. Also, ask if it's okay to use an older version of the textbook. Many times, the latest version isn't much different than a previous version, and the older version will cost a lot less. Sometimes the entire text of an older version is available online for free.

Then use one of the following sites to find the best deals on buying or renting textbooks or e-textbooks:

- Amazon.com (search for the textbook store)
- Bkstr.com
- CampusBooks.com
- eCampus.com
- Half.eBay.com (click on the "Textbooks" tab)
- Alibris.com (click on the "Textbooks" tab)
- AbeBooks.com (click on the "Textbooks" tab)

- BetterWorldBooks.com (click on the "Textbooks" tab)—this site will donate a book to someone in need for every book you buy
- ThriftBooks.com (click on the "Textbooks" tab)
- Chegg.com
- BookRenter.com

There are also textook cost-comparison search engines that will help you find the least expensive textbooks:

- BigWords.com
- BookFinder.com

Food

You'll probably use a meal plan at your dorm at least for your first couple of years, but there will likely be some options based on how frequently you plan to eat in the cafeteria. Think realistically about how many meals you'll be eating there each week and choose accordingly.

If you move on to an apartment at some point in your college career, get in the habit of planning ahead for what you'll make for dinner over the coming week. Then make your grocery list before going to the store, and try different stores to see which ones have the best prices for the items you buy most often. You'll find that some items are a lot less expensive at such stores as Target, Walmart, and Aldi.

Check out the many great coupon websites online, such as

CouponMom.com. They make it relatively easy to find coupons for items that are on sale at stores near you.

Here are some good sites that will help you with low-cost recipes:

- FrugalCuisine.blogspot.com
- FrugalFoodie.blogspot.com
- HungryForAMonth.blogspot.com
- Epicurious.com

Clothing

Many discount clothing stores offer great prices on brand-name clothing. Another great place to shop is secondhand stores. The Goodwill store close to where we live sells plenty of brand-new clothing, either items people never wore or unsold items dropped off by department stores.

In addition, "shop" your closet. I've heard that the average person regularly wears only 20 percent of the clothing in his or her closet. That sounds about right. So the next time you feel like you absolutely need something new, take a look inside your closet before heading to the store. Chances are that you will find something you haven't worn in a while that still fits and still looks good.

Clothing swaps have also become popular. These are events where everyone brings items they no longer want and then swaps them for other items free of charge. Consider organizing one at your dorm or church.

Lastly, buy clothing that does not require dry cleaning.

Household/Personal

One of the most important categories here is gifts. Because gift giving tends to ebb and flow throughout the year, make a list of all the people you plan to buy gifts for this year. Then set an annual gift budget, divide by twelve, and put that amount into your savings account for periodic bills and expenses each month. You'll find this especially helpful at Christmas, since that's when a lot of people who did not plan ahead end up going into debt buying Christmas presents.

Entertainment/Dining Out

There are probably lots of free things to do on your campus: concerts, talks, and more. And your student ID card can score you discounts on restaurant meals, bus or train tickets, museum tickets, concerts, electronic gear, and more. If it isn't clear whether a certain store offers student discounts, ask.

Cable or satellite television is not a utility expense; it is entertainment. Consider lower-cost packages or go without such services. If you have an older television, you can buy a digital-signal converter box at an electronics store, or if you have a newer television, it should be able to pick up the free digital signals from nearby television stations. Today, many programs are available at no or low cost through the Internet.

Groupon and other daily-deal sites can save you money. Just don't succumb to what I call financial death by discount. That's where you end up spending more than you would normally because all those deals seem like such bargains. The key is setting a budgeted amount for entertainment each month. Then when you know you have $20 to spend at a restaurant this weekend and you find a deal that enables you to spend just $15, that's a true deal.

Another great source for restaurant discounts is Restaurant .com, which regularly offers $25 certificates for specific restaurants for $10. But don't ever spend that much, because if you give them your e-mail address, you will often receive coupon codes where you can purchase $25 certificates for just $2. There are usually restrictions as to what nights the discounts are available and certain minimum-purchase requirements, but if you're going out to eat anyway, you might as well see if a discount certificate is available.

Another good source for restaurant discounts for college students is CampusSpecial.com.

When was the last time you visited your local library? Besides books, libraries have movies on DVD, music CDs, computers with Internet access, and sometimes even free tickets to museums, zoos, and music venues near you.

As you can see, there are lots of options for discounted entertainment.

Miscellaneous

Everyone incurs expenses that defy definition, so budget at least $25 per month for miscellaneous expenses.

Surf to Save

When shopping for something that is sold in more than one store, use a comparison-shopping website, such as Shopping.com or PriceGrabber.com, to see who has the best price.

For everything from rental cars to electronics, you should be able to double-dip on discounts; sometimes you can even triple-dip. I'm in the habit of first looking for a discount code at RetailMeNot.com. Then I go to Ebates.com and enter the retailer's website from there. By using both sites, I get a discount on the purchase and also a little money back in the form of a rebate check. A discount can be a good thing; two or three discounts on a single purchase are even better.

Recently I triple-dipped when buying tires for our vehicle. I researched the type of tires I wanted to buy, discovered that Sears was offering a $70 rebate, found an additional $5 off coupon code online, and then made the purchase online (while setting up an appointment for installation) after entering the Sears site through Ebates, which generated an additional $20 rebate.

The Savings Will Add Up

Start putting the ideas in this chapter into action and you'll improve the effectiveness of your spending in every category. Remember, these ideas are not about obsessive frugality; they're about spending smart so you have more money to give away and save. For a steady stream of new ideas about spending wisely, subscribe to the blog at SoundMindInvesting.com.

Memory Verse

If you have not been trustworthy in handling worldly wealth, who will trust you with true riches? (Luke 16:11)

Reflection Question

1. When you spend money, how often do you think about the fact that it's really God's money you're spending? How much will that reminder change how you spend?

Action Step

Fill in the rest of the *Cash Flow Plan*, using the spending categories that are relevant to you. Decide how much you can afford to put toward those things, knowing that 50 percent of the money you'll bring in each month is already spoken for (remember, 10 percent for giving and 40 percent for savings).

13

Living a Nonconforming Life

Do not conform any longer to the pattern of this world, but be transformed by the renewing of your mind. Then you will be able to test and approve what God's will is — his good, pleasing and perfect will.

ROMANS 12:2

There are two great days in our lives: the day we are born and the day we discover why.

JOHN MAXWELL

The film *Seabiscuit* is the true story of a Depression-era racehorse that was too small, a jockey who was too big, a trainer who was too old, and an owner who was "too dumb to know the difference."[1] It's a story about identity.

When Seabiscuit was born, his first owner didn't think much of him and used him to train others. In order to give the other horses confidence, the jockey riding Seabiscuit would pull back on the reins near the finish line to let the other horse win. Seabiscuit was conditioned to lose.

By the time another trainer, Tom Smith, got his first look at Seabiscuit, the horse had become angry and uncooperative. But Smith saw potential in him and persuaded Charles Howard, his boss, to buy the horse.

In one powerful scene, Smith and Howard are watching Seabiscuit resist the commands of its jockey as the horse runs this way and that around a track. Sensing Howard's concern, Smith tells him, "I just can't help feeling they got him so screwed up running in a circle he's forgotten what he was born to do. He just needs to learn how to be a horse again."[2] So they take him to a meadow and let him run. And run he does, fast and free.

Some of us have been so messed up by the messages of our consumer culture that we've forgotten what we were born to do. We've bought into the lies that we don't have enough, that we are not enough, that we need something more in order to be more. We just need to learn how to be children of God again.

Of course, there's nothing wrong with buying things. Biblical money management is not about making do with the least expensive car, clothes, or living room couch. But there's a lot that's wrong with looking to such things for our identity, value, and ultimate happiness. When we do, we settle for life on a treadmill of buying and wanting and wondering why we always seem to need something more. It goes a long way toward explaining why so many of us get into trouble with debt.

Remembering who we are — fully loved children of God — is the first and most essential habit of the steward's heart. It's what enables us to cultivate four attitudes that are essential for wise money management: trust, contentment, gratitude, and patience.

Trust

In December of 2006, as each week brought news of yet another publisher that had decided to take a pass on a book I had left a well-paying corporate job to write, I found myself discouraged and increasingly worried. Was it a colossal mistake to walk away from a good salary and benefits? Had God really called me to write and teach about biblical money management full-time, or was it simply something I wanted to do? Would I be able to provide for my wife and young children?

At the end of one especially discouraging day, my wife, Jude, and I were driving to the home of some friends for dinner. I was doing my best to hold it together. Knowing how down I was, she reminded me of the question asked in Matthew 7:

> If your children ask for bread, which of you would give them a stone? Or if your children ask for a fish, would you give them a snake? Even though you are bad, you know how to give good gifts to your children. How much more your heavenly Father will give good things to those who ask him! (verses 9–11, NCV)

The words felt like such a warm embrace that I could not speak. They were at once so reassuring and so humbling. In my worry, I had doubted God's promise to provide for us. Even worse, I had doubted his love for me.

As Jude and I talked that night, we agreed there was no

guarantee I would ever find a publisher, but there *was* a guarantee that God would provide for our needs. And he did. Five months later, NavPress offered me a book contract, and a year and a half later, my first book (*Money, Purpose, Joy*) was released. I remember being in a meeting at the publisher's office in Colorado Springs and finding it difficult to focus on the conversation. I couldn't help thinking back on the journey, and I was overwhelmed by God's goodness.

Whenever we find ourselves worrying about something, that's a good time to stop and pray. God's Word encourages us to do so: "Cast all your anxiety on him because he cares for you" (1 Peter 5:7). Have any financial concerns, such as paying for college, been weighing on your mind? Take a minute to remember that the God of the universe—the Creator of heaven, earth, and sea—considers you his child. He knows your needs and promises to provide for you.

Contentment

Every day of our lives, we are the unwitting recipients of countless messages designed to foster discontentment. The environments we move through have become so embedded with marketing messages that we hardly even notice them. That's what makes them so effective.

If we passed a billboard explicitly stating that a certain brand of clothing would make us popular, we'd immediately identify the lie. But the messages are not that explicit; they're woven tightly into the fabric of our everyday experience, which enables them to shape us in ways we don't recognize. For the most part, they leave us feeling that we need something more, which is what makes the following verses seem so out of synch with our daily lives: "Godliness with contentment is great gain. For we brought nothing into the world, and we can take nothing out of it. But if we have food and clothing, we will be content with that" (1 Timothy 6:6-8).

What? Content with only food and clothing? Why, that's downright un-American! Or so it seems. But do you know what else it is? It's liberating.

A few years ago, my wife and I gave away my car. Until it developed the need for a cost-prohibitive repair, the car was running fine, but it sure didn't look attractive. We used to live in a part of Chicago where we had to park it on the street, and it had been hit several times. The week before we moved from that neighborhood, a tree branch fell on the car, denting the roof. Because of its high mileage, we never bothered to fix any of the dents. When I was working in corporate America, I would drive into the parking lot of my office building and pass lots of new cars. Driving the old Camry gave me frequent opportunities to practice contentment.

What helped me the most was reminding myself that the car gave us the financial freedom to build savings targeted toward being able to leave my corporate job one day to write and speak full-time. The more I dwelled on that benefit, the more thankful I felt for a car that was paid off and that didn't cost much to operate. In the process, I saw that gratitude drives contentment, and contentment is perhaps the most powerful antidote to our culture's constant encouragement to want something more.

Gratitude

Writer Fulton Oursler had vivid memories of an old woman named Anna, who raised him as a child. When she sat down to eat, she would say, "Much obliged, dear Lord, for my vittles." Oursler wondered why she thanked God, pointing out that she would get the food regardless of whether she gave thanks or not.

"Sure, but it makes everything taste better to be thankful," Anna said. "You know, it's a game an old preacher taught me to play. It's about looking for things to be thankful for. Like one day I was walking to the store to buy a loaf of bread. I look in all the windows. There are so many pretty clothes."

"But, Anna, you can't afford to buy any of them!" he interjected.

"Oh, I know, but I can play dolls with them. I can imagine your mom and sister all dressed up in them, and I'm thankful. Much obliged, dear Lord, for playing in an old lady's mind."

Many years later, when Anna was dying, Oursler stood by her bedside. "Her old hands were knotted together in a desperate clutch. Poor old woman," he thought. "What had she to be thankful for now? She opened her eyes and looked at me. 'Much obliged, dear Lord, for such fine friends.'"[3]

Being thankful is not about looking at life through rose-colored glasses or putting on an artificial smile no matter what we're going through. According to the Reverend Dr. John Westerhoff, who tells Anna's story in *Grateful and Generous Hearts*, gratitude is about viewing all of life as a gift. "Taking nothing for granted, demanding nothing as her due, [Anna] recognized that we come into this world with nothing, we go out with nothing, and in between we are given all we have." [4]

Right now, gratitude may be the last thing you feel. That's where I was in the early part of 2005. I was grieving and worn out from doing the best I could to help my parents through long illnesses that claimed my mother's life in December of 2003 and my father's in November of 2004. At the time, the worship team at our church frequently sang "Blessed Be Your Name." For a song that includes the lyrics "You give and take away," its up-tempo rhythm always struck me as wrong. I grew to dislike that song. I could not sing along.

With the passing of time, the pain of my parents' deaths has eased. Gradually, my sense of loss has been replaced by gratitude for having parents I deeply loved and respected. When the worship team sang that song recently, it wasn't until it was over that I realized I had sung all of the lyrics without hesitation.

No matter what's happening in your life, can you praise God for the blessings? Look for little things. Develop the habit of expressing thanks on a regular basis and you'll discover that a grateful heart is a great help in managing money well for the long haul.

Patience

In the late 1960s, Stanford University researchers conducted an experiment among hundreds of four-year-olds. One at a time, the children were brought into a room and told they could eat one treat (such as a marshmallow) right away, or if they could wait until the researcher returned from a brief errand, they could then have two.

A few kids couldn't wait at all. Before the researcher had even finished giving the instructions, the treat was gone. The majority of kids held out for an average of just three minutes. About 30 percent were able to resist temptation, waiting the fifteen minutes the researcher was gone in order to get the better reward.

Some twelve years later, when the kids were in high school, lead researcher Walter Mischel tracked them down again. He asked their parents, teachers, and academic advisors about the kids' abilities to plan and think ahead, cope with problems, and get along with peers. He also requested their SAT scores.

What he found was amazing. The kids who were not able to wait had more behavioral problems at school and home. They struggled in stressful situations, often had trouble paying attention, and found it difficult to maintain friendships.

As for their SAT scores, the kids who could wait fifteen minutes scored an average 210 points higher than the kids who could wait only thirty seconds.[5]

Clearly, good things really do come to those who wait. So helpful is the ability to delay gratification that psychologists call it the master principle. They say it is the most essential psychological skill for effective living.

Think about the financial benefits of patience. Those who routinely save for what they want instead of impatiently buying today on credit save thousands of dollars on interest. Those who patiently invest over long periods of time stand a much better chance of being able to save enough money for their own retirement.

The marshmallow-experiment kids who could wait were the ones who clearly saw that their future reward would be much better than the immediate reward. Having no doubt that the waiting would be worthwhile motivated them to be patient.

The apostle Paul said something very similar about heaven. He said that everyone who has placed their faith in Christ has "the firstfruits of the Spirit" (Romans 8:23), meaning that the presence of the Holy Spirit gives us a glimpse of heaven. And he said that this taste of our future inheritance naturally leads to two responses: a yearning for heaven and the patience to wait for that reward (see Romans 8:22-25).

Do you yearn for heaven? When I first thought about that, I had to admit that I don't. When I travel, I yearn to see my family. In the spring, I yearn for our summer vacation. As for heaven? I'm thankful that it's real, but I can't say I'm in any hurry to get there.

If it seems that you don't yearn for heaven either, maybe you actually do. Think about something you love to do: your favorite hobby, perhaps, or a place where you love to vacation. C. S. Lewis said that our longing to spend more time doing what we most enjoy is an expression of our ultimate longing for heaven. He wrote,

> It [is] not *in* them, it only [comes] *through* them, and what [comes] through them [is] longing. . . . For they are not the thing itself; they are only the scent of a flower we have not found, the echo of a tune we have not heard, news from a country we have never yet visited.[6]

That's why even the best things of this world only leave us wanting more. As Lewis wrote, "If I find in myself a desire which no experience of this world can satisfy, the most probable explanation is that I was made for another world."[7]

The realization that the things of this world will never completely satisfy our deepest longings is not bad news; it's good news. It helps us stop looking to them for what they are incapable of delivering, and it frees us to enjoy them for what they are: good gifts from God but not the basis of our identity, security, and ultimate happiness.

The patience to wait for our ultimate reward in heaven is what turns the master principle into *the Master's principle.*

As John Eldredge wrote, we express our longing for God best when we "enjoy what there is now to enjoy, while waiting with eager anticipation for the feast to come."[8]

Are you looking to something of this world to deliver what only heaven can deliver? The clearer you are about what the things of this world can deliver and what only heaven can deliver, the more your use of money will be transformed.

Be Intentional

These habits of the heart—trust, contentment, gratitude, patience—will not just happen, nor will the habit of embracing our identity as children of God. They will take some tending, some reminding.

In order to cultivate these habits of the heart, be intentional about spending time with God. Read Matthew 7:9-11 again and again. Be awed, as John was, by the notion that the God of the universe considers you to be his child (see 1 John 3:1). Look and see how he has provided for you. Practice contentment by looking for things to be thankful for, such as being stuck at the end of a long line, which gives you the opportunity to practice patience!

To accept the cultural suggestion that you are a consumer is to settle for far too little. You were made in the image of the God of the universe (see Genesis 1:26-27). You were made for a life of good works prepared in advance for you to do (see Ephesians 2:10). You were made to love God and people well (see Matthew 22:36-40). Allow these truths to permeate your heart, and your use of money will become a powerful, productive, joyful, God-glorifying expression of who you were made to be and what you were made to be about. It is the single most important step you can take toward managing money well for the rest of your life.

APPENDIX

- Monthly Cash Flow Plan
- Cash Flow Tracker
- Recommended Spending Guide

Monthly Cash Flow Plan

Monthly Income	Now	Goal		Now	Goal
Monthly Income			**Taxes**		
Job (gross)	____	____	Federal	____	____
Parents/other	____	____	State	____	____
			Social Security (FICA)	____	____
Giving	____	____	Medicare	____	____
Charity _____	____	____	Other	____	____
Charity _____	____	____			
			Food	____	____
Savings	____	____	**Clothing**	____	____
Emergency fund	____	____			
< 5 yr. goal _____	____	____	**Household/Personal**	____	____
			Dry cleaning	____	____
Debts	____	____	Gifts	____	____
Credit Card	____	____	Furniture/household items	____	____
Credit Card	____	____	Cosmetics	____	____
Credit Card	____	____	Barber/beauty	____	____
Car/Truck Loan	____	____	Allowances	____	____
Education	____	____	Education (textbooks, etc.)	____	____
Other	____	____			
			Entertainment	____	____
Investing	____	____	Restaurants/movies	____	____
Retirement	____	____	Cable/satellite TV	____	____
College	____	____	Vacation	____	____
> 5 yr. goal _____	____	____	Books/subscriptions	____	____
			Health club/hobbies	____	____
Housing	____	____	Pets	____	____
Mortgage/rent	____	____			
Real estate tax	____	____	**Health**	____	____
Property insurance	____	____	Medical/dental insurance	____	____
			Prescriptions/co-pays	____	____
Maintenance/Utilities	____	____	Health savings account	____	____
Maintenance	____	____	Disability insurance	____	____
Electric	____	____	Life insurance	____	____
Gas	____	____			
Water/Garbage	____	____	**Professional Services**	____	____
Home phone/Internet	____	____	Legal/accounting	____	____
Cell phone	____	____	Counseling	____	____
			Other	____	____
Transportation	____	____			
Gas	____	____	**Miscellaneous**	____	____
Vehicle maintenance	____	____			
Insurance	____	____	**Total Monthly Income**	____	____
Bus/train/parking/tolls	____	____	**Total Monthly Outgo**	____	____
License/fees	____	____	**Income Minus Outgo**	____	____

Cash Flow Tracker

Month _____

	Income	Giving	Savings	Debts	Investing	Housing	Trans.	Maint./Utilities	Taxes	Food	Clothing	HH/Pers.	Ent.	Health	Prof. Svs.	Misc.
Cash Flow Plan																
Total																
(Over)/Under Vs. Plan																
Last Month YTD																
Total YTD																

1 | 2 | 3 | 4 | 5 | 6 | 7 | 8 | 9 | 10 | 11 | 12 | 13 | 14 | 15 | 16 | 17 | 18 | 19 | 20 | 21 | 22 | 23 | 24 | 25 | 26 | 27 | 28 | 29 | 30 | 31

Recommended Spending Guide
(One-Person Household)

Annual Gross Income	$30,000		$45,000		$60,000	
Monthly Gross Income	$2,500		$3,750		$5,000	
Giving	$250	10.0%	$375	10.0%	$500	10.0%
Saving/Investing	$250	10.0%	$412	11.0%	$600	12.0%
Consumer Debts	0	0.0%	0	0.0%	0	0.0%
Housing	$625	25%	$919	24.5%	$1,175	23.5%
Maintenance/Utilities	$150	6.0%	$206	5.5%	$250	5.0%
Transportation	$225	9.0%	$262	7.0%	$300	6.0%
Income Taxes	$405	16.2%	$652	17.4%	$915	18.3%
Food	$250	10.0%	$319	8.5%	$350	7.0%
Clothing	$30	1.2%	$75	2.0%	$150	3.0%
Other HH/Personal	$30	1.2%	$75	2.0%	$100	2.0%
Entertainment	$50	2.0%	$94	2.5%	$175	3.5%
Health	$200	8.0%	$300	8.0%	$350	7.0%
Professional Svcs.	$10	0.4%	$38	1.0%	$50	1.0%
Miscellaneous	$25	1.0%	$23	0.6%	$25	0.5%
Discretionary	$0	0.0%	$0	0.0%	$60	1.2%
Total	$2,500	100%	$3,750	100%	$5,000	100%

NOTES

Chapter 1: Your Future Is Amazingly Bright

1. "2011 RCS Fact Sheet #3: Age Comparisons Among Workers," Retirement Confidence Survey, http://ebri.org/pdf/surveys/rcs/2011/FS3_RCS11_Age _FINAL1.pdf.

2. Mindy Fetterman and Barbara Hansen, "Young People Struggle to Deal with Kiss of Debt," *USA Today*, http://www.usatoday.com/money/perfi/ credit/2006-11-19-young-and-in-debt-cover_x.htm.

Chapter 2: The Habits of Financial Wisdom

1. Malcom Gladwell, *Outliers: The Story of Success* (New York: Little, Brown, 2008), 47.

2. See Proverbs 3:5.

3. See Jeremiah 29:11.

Chapter 3: Habit One: Remembering Who You Are

1. William Leach, *Land of Desire: Merchants, Power, and the Rise of a New American Culture* (New York: Vintage, 1993), 9.

2. Susan Strasser, *Satisfaction Guaranteed: The Making of the American Mass Market* (Washington, DC: Smithsonian Books, 1995), 15.

3. Strasser, 89.

4. Juliet B. Schor, *The Overworked American: The Unexpected Decline of Leisure* (New York: Basic Books, 1992), 119.

5. Leach, 3.

6. *Confessions of a Shopaholic*, directed by P. J. Hogan (Burbank, CA: Touchstone Home Entertainment, 2009), DVD.

Chapter 4: Habit Two: Planning to Succeed

1. Thomas J. Stanley and William D. Danko, *The Millionaire Next Door: The Surprising Secrets of America's Wealth* (New York: Pocket Books, 1996), 41.

Chapter 5: Habit Three: Learning to Earn

1. Doug Lederman, "The Impact of Student Employment," *Inside Higher Ed*, June 8, 2009, http://www.insidehighered.com/news/2009/06/08/work.

2. *About Schmidt*, directed by Alexander Payne (Los Angeles: New Line Home Entertainment, 2003), DVD.

3. Martin Seligman, *Authentic Happiness: Using the New Positive Psychology to Realize Your Potential for Lasting Fulfillment* (New York: The Free Press, 2002), 168.

4. Erin White, "Corporate Tuition Aid Appears to Keep Workers Loyal," *Wall Street Journal*, May 21, 2007, B4.

Chapter 6: Habit Four: Giving Some Away

1. "Press Release: UNICEF's State of The World's Children report commemorates 20 years of the Convention on the Rights of the Child," UNICEF, November 19, 2009, http://www.unicef.org/rightsite/sowc/pdfs/Embargoed_Press_Release_SOWC_19_November_2009_EN.pdf.

2. David Myers, *The Pursuit of Happiness* (New York: Morrow, 1992), 194–195.

Chapter 7: Habit Five: Putting Some Away

1. Matt Bell, "Tough Times Call for a Return to the Basics of Wise Money Management," December 21, 2008, http://www.mattaboutmoney.com/uploads/Financial-Stress.pdf.

Chapter 10: Habit Eight: Playing Great Offense

1. "MFS Investment Sentiment Survey Offers Insight into Generation Y Investing Behaviors" MFS, September 6, 2011, https://www.mfs.com.

Chapter 12: Habit Ten: Spending Smart

1. Juliet B. Schor, *The Overspent American: Why We Want What We Don't Need* (New York: HarperPerennial, 1998), 57.

Chapter 13: Living a Nonconforming Life

1. The Internet Movie Database dialogue found here: http://www.imdb.com/title/tt0329575/quotes.
2. *Seabiscuit*, directed by Gary Ross (Universal City, CA: Universal Studios, 2003), DVD.
3. Dr. John H. Westerhoff, "Grateful and Generous Hearts" (Atlanta: St. Luke's Press, 1997), 4–5.
4. Westerhoff, 5.
5. "Marshmallows and 'Grit,'" http://www.princetonacademy.org/weblogs/heads-journal/archives/Images/Microsoft%20Word%20-%20Olen's%20letter.pdf.
6. C. S. Lewis, *The Weight of Glory* (New York: HarperCollins, 2001), 30–31.
7. C. S. Lewis, *Mere Christianity* (New York: HarperCollins, 2001), 136–137.
8. Brent Curtis and John Eldredge, *The Sacred Romance: Drawing Closer to the Heart of God* (Nashville: Thomas Nelson, 1997), 199.

ABOUT THE AUTHOR

MATT BELL is a personal-finance writer and speaker and author of *Money, Purpose, Joy*; *Money Strategies for Tough Times*; *Freed-Up from Debt*; and *Money and Marriage*. He speaks at churches, universities, conferences, and other venues throughout the country. Matt has been quoted in *USA Today*, *U.S. News & World Report*, the *Chicago Tribune*, and *Kiplinger's Personal Finance* magazine and has been a guest on WGN-TV and several nationally syndicated radio talk shows. He holds a master's degree in interdisciplinary studies from DePaul University, where he wrote a thesis about the emergence of America's consumer culture and its influence on people's beliefs and behaviors. Matt lives with his wife and their three young children in the Chicago area. To learn more about his work and subscribe to his blog, go to MattAboutMoney.com and SoundMindInvesting.com.

MY LIFE IS **TOUGHER** THAN MOST **PEOPLE REALIZE.**

I TRY TO KEEP EVERYTHING *IN BALANCE:* FRIENDS, FAMILY, WORK, SCHOOL, AND GOD.

IT'S NOT EASY.

I KNOW WHAT MY PARENTS BELIEVE AND WHAT MY PASTOR SAYS.

BUT IT'S NOT ABOUT THEM. IT'S ABOUT ME...

ISN'T IT TIME I OWN MY FAITH?

THROUGH THICK AND THIN, KEEP YOUR HEARTS AT ATTENTION, IN ADORATION BEFORE CHRIST, YOUR MASTER. BE READY TO SPEAK UP AND TELL ANYONE WHO ASKS WHY YOU'RE LIVING THE WAY YOU ARE, AND ALWAYS WITH THE UTMOST COURTESY. 1 PETER 3:15 (MSG)

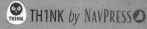

www.navpress.com | 1-800-366-7788   TH1NK by NAVPRESS